Let Me Tell You Something

J.A. Lovelock

Michael Terence Publishing

First published in paperback by
Michael Terence Publishing in 2019
www.mtp.agency

Copyright © 2019 J.A. Lovelock

J.A. Lovelock has asserted the right to be identified as the
author of this work in accordance with the
Copyright, Designs and Patents Act 1988

ISBN 9781913289065

No part of this publication may be reproduced, stored in a retrieval
system, or transmitted, in any form or by any means, electronic,
mechanical, photocopying, recording or otherwise, without the prior
permission of the publishers

Cover background image
Copyright © Alekss

Cover author image
FocalPoint Studios

Cover design
Copyright © 2019 Michael Terence Publishing

For my soldier boy
My life and my love
Always

For my grandfather Benjamin
For my grandmother Ethel
who saw what I could become
Bless you

Go confidently in the direction of your dreams!

Live the life you've imagined.

- Henry Thoreau

Contents

Foreword 1
What Others are Saying about J.A. Lovelock 3
Introduction 7
WOMEN! 9
SCAMS, SCANDALS AND THE LIKE 17
PIGS MIGHT FLY – TRAVEL STORIES 27
THE SHORT ARM OF THE LAW 37
And Now For a Brief Intermission 53
History Will Tell 57
Top Flight 60
MEN! 64
LONDON TOWN 68
(INTA)RACIAL RELATIONS 73
TOO POOR TO BREED 87
ALL IN A DAY'S WORK 88
FAMILY MATTERS 96
LET'S GET POLITICAL 106
CHRISTMAS A COME 110
AND ANOTHER THING… 113

Foreword

Most of these sketches were first published in the *Jamaican Times UK* and already have a prestigious seal of approval, but nonetheless, I am pleased to add my 'two-penny bit' worth to borrow a phrase from 'Let Me Tell You Something'.

Firstly, these humorous sketches, though based on topical events and issues in the public eye at the time of first publication, are timeless in their appeal, so any lapse of time since they were written is of little consequence. They still come off the page fresh and as appealing as when first written.

The sketches are a delicious mixture of editorial, gossip column and cartoon appeal in their pithy humour and insight into that wide gamut of human fate and folly. The language used is breezy and accessible, and though you need not be Jamaican to enjoy the occasional colloquialism, it does add a touch of piquancy if they remind you of 'home'.

You might be forgiven for thinking that these sketches with their light, comic touch won't tread on serious matters, but just every now and again we are reminded that J.A. Lovelock is not afraid of tackling controversial, contentious matters, and their entertaining quality is often a mask for matters of grave public concern.

Of special appeal throughout is the inevitably universal theme of human relationships and these are hilariously explored under such headings as:

'WOMEN',

'MEN!'

'SCAMS, SCANDALS AND THE LIKE',

'PIGS MIGHT FLY – TRAVEL STORIES'.

So there you have it, fasten your seat belts and prepare for *nuff* belly laughs!

- Errol Lloyd, London 2019

What Others are Saying about J.A. Lovelock and Let Me Tell You Something

J.A. Lovelock's British-Jamaican take on life, love and laughter. Warm-hearted, common-sense, and enjoyable to read.

- **Maggie Gee OBE**, *award-winning Author and Professor of Creative Writing, Bath Spa University*

Let Me Tell You Something, as well as being a thought-provoking narrative on the dangers of 21st Century life, is an illustration of the unique Jamaican sense of humour, which can be expressed in Jamaican patois in a way it cannot be accurately expressed in English.

These highly recommended stories are a humorous, tongue in cheek and enlightening glimpse of modern life and its many pitfalls under a microscope; touching on almost every event which has hit headlines in recent years.

I began to read the first story 'Women', which immediately drew me in and held my attention, only putting it down to laugh out loud. The 'Travel Stories' were an eye-opener. I will be carrying disinfectant wipes and pig scarers in future when I fly!

- Deanne Heron, *Poet and award-winning Author of Pardner Money stories, a collection of short humorous stories about Jamaican culture*

Often polemic without breaking into a full-on rant, frequently charming in their slice-of-life narrative and always whip-crack sharp in delivery, the columns seem to sprout from tiny seeds of thought and grow into fully fledged messages. Lovelock has this great habit of luring a reader in with humour before giving them something to think about long after the piece is read. Her voice is sassy, witty, beguiling and extremely personable. There is something beyond the tone… something erudite, learned, patient and purposeful… a fascinating mix… a spunky woman with razor-shape teeth that are made of brain power.

J.A. Lovelock seems like a bit of modern-day folk hero, one championing common sense and lampooning idiocy where-ever it may be found.

- Melrose Books

J.A. Lovelock is one of London's most engaging columnists and an accomplished purveyor of this sadly diminishing journalistic art. Sometimes provocative, sometimes outspoken but always witty and entertaining, this collection of her writings is an absolute delight.

- Simon Corbin, *Author, Copywriter, Lecturer in Journalism & Creative Writing*

An entertaining, thought-provoking and sometimes controversial collection of columns on an eclectic range of subjects, from scams to hospital parking charges to the fashion for large buttocks. J.A. Lovelock's lively style and distinctive voice seamlessly blends Jamaican and British cultural references in a way that makes her writing accessible to all.

- **Sandra Hempel,** *award-winning Author of The Inheritor's Powder*

Lovelock pulls you in from the onset…various anecdotes from news stories entwined with her wit do enable her to transmute some concerning discourses of this compilation to more light-hearted reading. If you want a stimulating talk show in a book with snippets of global travel, well here is the perfect piece of writing. Readers will begin to understand the Jamaican humour, the patois is the heartbeat of the writing, yet this work will relate to a wider diverse audience. A good read that will guarantee you to laugh a lot.

- **Amanda Epe** - *Multiple award-winning Author of A Fly Girl*

Introduction

Dear Reader

Hello and welcome to *Let Me Tell You Something*. I would, first of all, like to offer special thanks to Andrew Clunis, Managing Editor, who gave me a column in the monthly published *Jamaica Times UK* which he titled 'Musings with Lovelock'. I have had much to muse about.

I have always wanted to be a columnist (largely because I like to opine and get my two-penny bit in!) and even though I had some experience in creative writing, wherein I largely fibbed, that is, made up stories, I feel that I would tell almost anyone I met that I wanted to be a columnist, and it was not for want of trying to get a newspaper editor to take me on. Some of the ones I contacted, the ones who bothered to reply, told me they would 'keep me on file'. Take that as a 'No, thanks'. But then along came Andrew. And here we are. And what a privilege it has been.

These pieces are not in chronological order and some have been adapted and extended from the column pieces.

There are also some pieces that did not appear in the column. I have arranged them so that you can dip in and out and read them any way you like and in any order that pleases you. I hope you enjoy reading them as much as I have enjoyed writing them. Thank you for reading this book.

- J.A. Lovelock

WOMEN!

When will they ever learn? Lonely British women that is. Yet again we hear a sorry tale that some women of a certain age have fallen for the charms of an online 'lover' whose only interest is to relieve them of their hard-earned dosh. These women don't just fall in love and give their hearts away willy-nilly to some stranger, but it seems they are just as eager to part with their money. The latest scammer is a Maurice Asola Fadola from Ghana who passed himself off as a dashing American major general, who charmed his unsuspecting victims with stories of his bravery dodging bombs and saving lives on the battlefield when nuttin' nuh go so! He scammed £800,000 out of his victims based on variations of this lie – like needing money to pay for a legal dispute to get his war medals and buying his way out of the army. What a load of tosh! Why would any self-respecting man who hadn't even met me want my money to bail him out? That's what I'd be asking. Doesn't he have friends or family? Why ask me? As a result of this conman's trickery, some women have been left penniless and homeless, some having re-mortgaged their homes to help out lover-boy. They won't be getting any sympathy from me. Where do these women get the idea anyway that they are supposed to give men money? Especially ones they have never clapped eyes on. But this *ginnal* Fadola, he did send them poetry. That's a red flag flying right there.

Now, I'm no meanie. I have given pennies for the guy in Bonfire season and I have rewarded carol singers who came a-wassailing with the odd shilling or two, but I have never given money to a man I was dating. Not even a bus fare. Giving money to a man you have never clapped eyes on? What were these women thinking? One day, brushing their teeth or lying in bed, they surely must have thought, "This isn't quite right", or "That's the third time he's asked me for money." Clearly, it did not occur to them that Fadola seemed oddly friendless and appeared to have no family.

And it doesn't end there. When an elderly Cardiff woman befriended a young waiter while on holiday in Tunisia, she told him that if he ever visited the UK he should drop in to see her. Well, there was an invite he could hardly refuse! It appears that even if he was on his way to Mars he would be sure to go via Cardiff, so as not to disappoint this old dear. Two twos our young Tunisian opportunist finds himself in Cardiff and takes up residence in the lady's house – and before you know, he has eaten her out of house and home. I have never been duped by any man in such ways, so there's no point in telling me that these misfortunes could befall anyone. As my mother used to say, "*duppy know who fi fright'n.*" And no duppy man is going to frighten me. All I can say is, you women of a certain age, wise up! And if you have any money you don't know what to do with, call me.

Take Michelle Christie. Take her, please. Mrs Christie is a widow woman whose husband recently passed away after losing his fight with cancer. She has written an open letter (published in a national daily paper) berating those friends and family who visited her and her dying husband bearing grapes (seedless of course), Lucozade and sympathy. Mrs Christie asserts that she did not appreciate all this goodwill, as it robbed her of precious time with her husband. She says that when her husband became ill it seemed "he became public property". She is having a right go at these kind-hearted and thoughtful neighbours who had bothered to show they cared. You ever hear anything go so? What an ungrateful so-and-so. Lots of people fall seriously ill and have neither kith nor kin to drop by with a bowl of chicken soup. Her actions will undoubtedly put people off showing up at such future occurrences for fear of being shown the door. Can you imagine it? This could be the end of 'nine-nights' as we know it. Fried fish, bammy and jerk chicken washed down by the free-flowing Wray & Nephew and Red Stripe that are customary on these occasions could soon become a distant memory. And future murmurings might consist of *'Member when Maas Ranny dead...?* On the other hand, bereaved relatives have been known to bemoan the fact that after such initial outpourings of support and sympathy, folk tend to fall away after the funeral and the food and rum are done. I am afraid, after her open letter to 'family, friends and acquaintances', well everybody, Mrs Christie might be wishing her visitors consisted of more than just the postman.

Chlorine and curls do not mix. That is a well-known universal truth. And that is why many black women won't go swimming if they can help it. It's the hair thing. As most black women use chemical relaxers in their hair, this makes hair susceptible to chlorine damage which can, over time, lead to hair loss. So if you are planning to take a dip in your local swimming pool you have to time it right, in between getting your hair done. You can't just get up and go on a whim. Consequently, a lot of black women (and men apparently) cannot swim – I being one of them. I like the idea of swishing and swooshing about in the water with gay abandon and so, every once in a while, I think about taking swimming lessons. Once or twice, I have ventured into a pool resplendent in armbands clutching my float which I kept, optimistically, from junior school days. I would really like to learn to swim, but now something is putting me off. A recent survey found that 70 per cent of people said they didn't shower before getting into the pool, thereby treating it as a communal bath; and worse, while in the pool they use it for all kinds of toilet purposes. Seems pretty disgusting to me and that has set me back. Get my own pool, eh!

***

Poor Dhakirah Salim. She is all upset because she was banned from entering a beauty contest. Why was she banned? Because she is a mother. Birmingham single mum of a three-year-old daughter, Ms Salim was directed by the organisers to the small print of the regional heat of Miss England which states mothers and married women were barred from entering the contest. Ms Salim bemoaned that the restriction is old-fashioned and should be changed. To suit her, presumably. I like the way people make their own rules about other people's business. I agree with the organisers for banning mothers. There is a lot to do in promoting these events: places to go to and people to see, and where does a busy mum find time to do that and take care of her child? Go sit-down Dhakirah!

***

When I was quite young I decided to save up as much money as I could get my paws on to pay for what I believed to be a much-needed and life-saving operation. You see, I was well-endowed in the derrière region and spent much of my life being embarrassed by it. Musicians used to write and sing songs about it. *Tek me mek poppy show*. For years I nursed the idea of undergoing surgery to reduce what I considered to be an affliction. So, imagine my shock when, over the past few years, the very thing I wanted to be rid of, women were actually paying money, serious money, to increase in size. What? I kid you not. The fulsome backside has become an object of beauty and desire and certainly came into its own thanks to the likes of Jennifer Lopez and Kim Kardashian. Furthermore, some women would go to great lengths, even deadly lengths, to acquire bigger buttocks. Take the case of Claudia Aderotimi, a 20-year-old university student and dancer from London who died following a botched buttock implant. Miss Aderotimi had flown to Philadelphia in 2011 to have the butt enhancement procedure, but sadly was given illegal silicone implants by fake surgeon Padge-Victoria Windslowe, who has recently been convicted of third-degree murder. By all accounts, it appears Miss Aderotimi was an attractive young lady with a bright and pleasing future, and it is a shame her life was cut short by feeling compelled to take such drastic steps to enhance her beauty. Steps that did nothing more than take her life. As for me, c'mon girl – shake that booty!

> *A pastor was raising funds for a new church roof. He said to the congregation, anyone who would give a £1000 could pick out the next three hymns. A little old lady in the back sprang to her feet and said, "Pastor, I will do it." The pastor thanked her, and said, which three hymns would you like? She looked around the congregation, pointed to three young men and said, "I'll take him, him and him."*

***

Just when you thought things couldn't get any lower there comes a story that a shameless ex-wife, a Miss Helen Tippet, is demanding a share of her ex-husband's six-figure compensation as part of their divorce settlement. The ex-husband, Andrew Kerslake, was sexually abused when he was a child, leaving him with emotional and physical damage. His abuser has been jailed and Mr Kerslake was awarded £175,000 by the Criminal Injuries Compensation Authority. Why in the world would she want any part of that money which even Mr

Kerslake describes as 'blood money'? Mr Kerslake himself hasn't even spent a penny of it on himself, choosing instead to invest it in a trust fund which he intends to leave to charity upon his death. What a joy she must have been to live with!

***

Former tennis champion Chris Evert has recently revealed that going through the menopause caused her to leave her husband of 18 years for another man. I don't know how that works. The clue is in the name Chris: men-o-pause.

Fiyah deh a musmus battam, im tink a kool breeze!

***

My family, particularly the ladies, have always looked years younger than their age. And when asked how we manage to look so young, we have always put it down to genetics. But now I know it could be down to the pomegranate or 'prom-gra-nat', as we used to call it back home. Scientists have discovered that – OK, I won't blind you with science – but suffice it to say that they found a 'miracle' youth supplement in the pomegranate that keeps you young and beautiful and can even make you live longer if you're not careless with your life. *But hear ya.* Back in Jamaica, we had not one, but two pomegranate trees in our yard. We would eat the seeds, because that's what they were, but they were nothing special. They weren't like your favourite fruit or anything. They were just there. But all the while, unbeknown to us, the pomegranate and its special anti-ageing ingredient was charging up our cells and keeping ageing at bay. All hail the prom-gra-nat!

One evening when I was home alone and with nothing better to do, I thought I would take a fleeting glance over the 'lonely hearts' column of a national newspaper. I was quite taken by some of the entries and take the liberty of sharing some of them with you. One woman wrote, "My ideal match would be a man I can trust and who is honest. By the way, my name is Myrtle." Another wrote, "I am 58 years old and called Peggy. I am tall and seeking a man who likes to look at me." Another said she was, "bubbly, outgoing lady, 74 years of age and likes clubbing." Whoah! Go girl! Another one who couldn't make her mind up said she liked staying in and going out. But some women can be really fussy, as one said she would like a man who is alive… and jolly. Men didn't fare much better in their search for that one true love. One wrote that he was seeking a lady friend who would go with him on day trips to Margate[1] and Alton Towers[2].

---

[1] *Margate is the seaside.*
[2] *Alton Towers, a theme park, generally visited by children.*

SCAMS, SCANDALS AND THE LIKE

I am not normally one to be scammed; I am far too smart for that. However, on one occasion I came pretty close. Like many people, I was seduced by an online 'free sample' ad, and being partial to a little freebie here and there, a free jar of moisturiser was very appealing. To get this 'free sample', though, I was asked to give my bank details, and at first, I wondered: what merry trick is this? The product was supposed to be free. Apparently, while the product was free, postage was not. OK. My bank balance could support a one-off £3.99 postage. Soon after clicking 'Send', I duly received my pot of gold and, in no time, would be looking like the beauty I should have been born. The merch arrived, and I set it to work. Shortly thereafter, however, cracks began to appear, and not just on my face. The company were looking to fleece me of nearly £80 a month for the cream. It was cleverly hidden in the very tiny small print. As soon as I realized what the game was, I phoned the company to cancel. To cut a long and frustrating story short, they agreed (reluctantly) to cancel the transaction and refunded all the money they had taken from my account. I realized that I was very lucky, for as many as 400 complaints a day are received by banks from people who have been scammed by 'free sample' ads, costing customers around £30,000 a day. So, be warned. It is said there is no such thing as a free lunch. In this case, there is no such thing as a 'free sample'.

※※※

What is it with oversized people that they want to start a fight when someone makes some innocuous comment about weight, or even makes a helpful suggestion for their benefit? Jamelia, pop-star, actress and a panellist on daytime talk show *Loose Women,* said something along the lines that stores should not stock clothes below or above a certain size and that overweight and underweight people should have 'specialist shops'. Size 18, Gemma Collins, she of *The Only Way is Essex* fame, weighed into Jamelia, branding her "cruel and cold" for saying plus-sized shoppers should be made to feel uncomfortable about their weight. Well, I do not think it is shopkeepers' job to make customers, of any size, feel uncomfortable, but the point Jamelia was making was that we should not be facilitating an unhealthy lifestyle. I get that. Being overweight can lead to serious health problems like high blood pressure, type-2 diabetes and various complications relating to these conditions, putting extra strain on our already struggling health service. Given that obesity is on the rise, you would have thought anything which persuades the seriously overweight to put down the pies and pick up some weights would be welcome. So, get over yourself, Gemma. Either embrace your voluminous proportions or do something about it.

***

A funny peculiar story doing the rounds is that teachers with Northern or Midlands accents need to shape up and be posher Southern. Middle-class heads ain't having regional and broad accents in *dem* schools because children don't understand it. What say? What about a new teacher turning up one day, bounces into the class full of eager waiting children and says to them, *"wha'gwan, me pickney dem?"*

***

Tory MP Nadine Dorries has come under fire yet again. In promoting her recent novel, which deals with, among other things, sexual abuse, she claims she was sexually abused as a child by the well-known vicar, (and magazine writer) James Cameron. And she didn't stop there. Not knowing that he died in 2011, she pretty much named and shamed him as a sexually abusive character in her book. Ms Dorries has been castigated for revealing her abusive experience. Some people said she was wrong to do so now, with one woman stating she, "can't imagine him (the Reverend Cameron) doing such a thing." I do worry when some women make these sweeping, ill-thought-out statements about certain men, assuring their innocence. How well do they really know them? Watching the reverend vicar attired in his religious finery on a Sunday morning delivering his homilies, and catch him at a mid-week Bible Study, is all you see of him. As with all abusers and paedophiles, he is unlikely to show his evil side in public. Abusers generally don't advertise for witnesses or call a press conference to witness their evil deeds. Many women (and men) who suffered sexual abuse in their childhood do feel a degree of shame and guilt and it takes many years and a lot of courage to talk about it, if at all. Let's not be too quick to defend the so-called honour of the abuser, nor to castigate a person who says they were abused. Very few people would make this kind of thing up.

***

I have now got the hang of this 'no free bags' business at the supermarkets, and when I leave the house, even if it is only to the Post Office, I am tooled-up with my bags; and I permanently have two shopping bags in my little rucksack, even if I am not planning to go grocery shopping. I learnt to do this the hard way. In the early days of the 'pay for bag' ruling, I would only go out with shopping bags if I were actually going grocery shopping. But as these things go, I often found myself going to the supermarkets without even thinking. In October I had booked tickets at my local theatre to see the National Theatre Live production of *Hamlet*. This was my evening out. Not intending to go shopping at all. Yet, I found myself going into a well-known supermarket and leaving with twelve frozen vegetarian sausages and a packet of wholemeal bread-rolls. Then it dawned on me that I needed a bag to put them in. However, I was not mentally prepared to spend an extra 5p on a bag that was free the day before. Not to be beaten, and not wanting to parade my sausages and rolls for the world to see, I grabbed a copy of the Evening Standard and wrapped my supper therein. Walking through London, carrying this thing like a new-born baby proved trickier than I had envisaged. After a while, the sausages started to defrost. And water running down my frontage. Not a good look. At the theatre, I hid them under my seat and the sausages became so defrosted that water was now running all around me. As I was sitting in the aisle seat, all patrons wishing to make full use of the interval had to go past me, with the water emanating from under my seat. Lesson learnt.

Hands up, those who know what 'sirtfoods' are? Well, if you knew that, you are better than me. It's the kind of word you have to say sl*ooo*wly. Real slow. I know what it is now but, for the uninitiated, 'sirtfoods' are a particularly superfood diet that not only promises to shed pounds off your physique but at £1,500 a throw it will definitely relieve you of the pounds in your pocket, too. And that's a weekly rate. This diet, favoured by the rich and famous, including the delicious Lorraine Pascal, cake-maker extraordinaire, consists of strawberries, buckwheat, rocket, kale, green tea, red peppers and capers. What a caper! I have all of these in my regular diet and at a fraction of the price. Then there's the book, of course. That would set you back another £8. This sort of thing makes me worried about getting rich. It might fry my brains.

If this wasn't tragic it would be funny. A man of the cloth flogging £1.99 olive oil he bought from Aldi to his parishioners as a 'miracle cure'. Self-styled 'Archbishop of Peckham', Gilbert Deya, who had some child trafficking issues with Kenya, was caught selling this stuff in his church shop at £5 a bottle. What cheek! He claimed the oil, which he personally anointed, was able to treat all kinds of maladies including serious ones like cancer, barrenness and HIV. This scam came to light when an undercover couple went to see him pretending the wife had cancer. Deya started the 'miracle cure' treatment by rubbing the oil on the woman's chest. Where else? The National Health Service warns that scams offering 'miracle cures' are surprisingly widespread and take in hundreds of thousands of Brits who are convinced that pills and potions will cure their baldness, impotence or weight problems. It warns that, at the very least, these scams are a waste of your money, and that they can also be dangerous. I have a small bottle of holy oil which was given to me by some church folk at a recent exhibition. I didn't pay for it, I hasten to add. I was instructed to rub it on my head diligently morning and night for two weeks. After which time the thing I was in great need of – more money – would flow like a river. Well, I am not holding my breath.

I thought slavery days were over. But clearly, I was wrong. Because a recent case involving a Whitehall civil servant and her husband (of all people) kept an African woman (is this a joke?) as a slave in their home for some considerable time.

Over a decade, in fact. The couple, Teresa and Joel Abu, kept Rashida Ajayi in 'oppressive servitude' and paid her about £300 per year for her domestic labour. When I hear stories like this I do wonder which planet these people are on. Have they not heard the news?

***

I like a good gossip. Don't we all? Love to talk 'bout people business. But I am actually finding it difficult to find many people to *labrish* with these days. Seems like everyone *gaan PC*. But hear this. Gossiping is good! And if you're not doing it you are missing out, according to professors at the University of Pavia in Italy. They discovered (don't ask me how) that having a good natter about others is good for your health as it releases oxytocin. Oxytocin, for the unscientific among us, is the pleasure or happy hormone. The body releases oxytocin during mother and child bonding, when we touch each other, and before and after sex. So if you are not involved in any of the above you can still get your oxytocin fix from a good gossip. So go on, treat yourself, talk 'bout everybody you know. *Itch up inna people business* (but if *dem* tump you down, don't call me!) *Me hear say Miss Mattie husband…*

***

Not too long ago I experienced a persistent and (I considered) aggressive ringing of my doorbell. I didn't answer it. I don't respond to aggression and if you are going to ring my bell (of any description) do it nicely. After what seemed an age the ringing ceased. Then I looked out of the window to see if I could catch the culprit. I saw a man walking away with a parcel under his arm. I got all excited thinking I had a surprise gift. So I let him in. As I reached out with sweaty hands to grab my gift he told me it wasn't mine. Whose, then? He proceeded to tell me that the parcel was for my neighbour. That being the case, what's he ringing my bell for? He asked me if I could keep it for them as they appeared to be out. I wasn't best pleased but being (good) neighbourly and all that I said OK. He said he would put a note in their door to tell them I had it. Three weeks later I still did! Cluttering up my hallway. People, listen to me. If you are going to order goods from Amazon (which I believe they can deliver within 24 hours), don't go cruising halfway around the world or take a hike up Everest. Stay home and collect your stuff. I had half a mind to open it and see if there was anything worth keeping. It made me wonder how long can you keep your neighbours' unclaimed parcel before it becomes lawfully yours?

***

It shouldn't be allowed. Travellers getting free parking at hospitals, that is. Going to hospital these days, either as a visitor or a patient, is an expensive business. And hospitals seem to be making more money than ever from parking fees. Can you believe that in 2016, hospitals in England collected more than £120 million pounds (and rising) in parking charges? And what do they do with this ginormous amount of dosh – they use it to maintain the car parks. Oh yeah? Anyway, back to the travellers. It has come to my notice that Irish travellers have been allowed to camp at a Manchester hospital for free while a relative recover from heart surgery. Camping for free? They saved themselves £15 per day! If everyone else must pay, why not them? Why the bias towards travellers? I have had some experience with travellers. It's not that they can't afford to pay. They have money. Whilst I don't agree with the charging of extortionate fees, if everybody who drives into a hospital car park must dig deep and fork out for the privilege, then so the travellers should. End this nonsense now!

***

Hear ye! Hear ye! The end of the launderette [*ye olde bagwashe*] is nigh. This is a sad state of affairs. I liked going down to the launderette. It's the only time I found me some peace and rest. Sitting there watching the clothes go around and round. And the wheeze at the end of spinning. Bliss. I don't go so often now as I'm one of the 97 per cent of homes that own a washing machine. But I tend to go if I am washing my heavies. Quilts, rugs and the like. Things happen down at the launderette and you are likely to see all walks of life parade before your eyes. Like school kids tucking into their after-school takeaways, druggies consuming their portion, and the odd bag lady catching up on her afternoon kip. And once I was waiting for my quilt to dry when I saw three youths altercating at the door of the launderette. One was brandishing a 10-inch knife at another asking for the money he'd loaned him. Jeepers! I was terrified that something nasty was going to happen, the launderette would be cordoned off and I wouldn't be able to get my quilt. But prayers were answered, and they moved their barney down the road. The launderette is a great place to hang out. It has pride of place in our hearts and nation. Even in *Eastenders,* the launderette has been the heart of the show, and who can forget that Levi's commercial when Nick Kamen stripped off his jeans in the launderette to put them in the wash?

PS. The boys later kissed and made up and there was no bloodshed.

PIGS MIGHT FLY – TRAVEL STORIES

As if flying wasn't scary enough, I am now that told the fold-down table I eat my child-portion meals off on the plane has as many germs on it as a rank and stinking lavatory seat. And if that's not worry enough, I might even find myself sitting next to a pig. Of the four-legged kind, I hasten to add. What am I talking about? On a flight between Connecticut and Washington, an American woman was removed from the plane because her 'emotional support animal', the pig in question refused to remain buckled in its seat, *kin puppa lick* and made a run for it. To cap it all, he did his business on the aeroplane floor. Imagine that! Now, where's my broomstick?

***

While I could not be described as a 'frequent flyer' I have had my share of domestic and international travel and I would like to think that when I do fly the airlines take my safety seriously. Since the atrocities of 9/11 we can all testify that getting on a plane is less than a pleasant experience nowadays. Airport staff appear less friendly and you would be lucky to get a smile out of them. I flew from London to Edinburgh on New Year's Eve and I was subjected to an intense search and body scan. I had heard about the body scan and, like many people, thought it might be a little intrusive. But it wasn't that bad and, besides, I am all for any procedure that will keep me safe while cruising 40,000 feet in the air. So, I was somewhat bemused to learn that retired teacher John Williams flew home from his holiday in Lanzarote back to Liverpool without a passport and with only his bus pass as his travel document. Worse, it was not the original bus pass but an emailed copy of it. Suffice it to say that passport control staff in Liverpool were less than pleased with how Mr Williams, who I am sure is a decent, law-abiding citizen who probably has never had so much as a parking ticket, managed to board an international flight without proper travel documents confirming his identity. As Mr Williams smilingly confided, he wouldn't even be allowed on a bus with a photocopy of his bus pass. If I were booked as a passenger on his flight, I would be sorely tempted to create a rumpus by insisting he did not fly on my plane. I value my life, even if airlines do not.

I don't know what it is about some Brits that, when they go to other people's countries, they disrespect their laws and customs and behave in the same ungodly way they behave at home. Eleanor Hawkins from Derby is one such person. During a visit to a Malaysian mountain, she (and some equally stupid friends) decided to strip naked and take photos. Where did she think she was, Brighton? Well, stripping off is one thing, but this she did on Mount Kinabalu, one of Malaysia's most sacred mountains; and this the Malaysians did not take too kindly to. Malaysia is a conservative Muslim country and they don't tolerate this kind of loose and lewd behaviour. Especially in public. I have been to Malaysia and I was briefed before I went on how to behave so as not to cause the indigenous people offence. And so I didn't. Miss Hawkins broke their law and for that, she was jailed. She is a convicted criminal yet, when she returned to the UK, she was treated like some sort of celebrity. When her flight landed at Heathrow, she was met by her parents in a private suite. Private suite? Passengers on the flight were ordered, yes ordered, to remain in their seats until she was escorted off the plane to avoid cameramen. Special treatment, or what? Expect to see her propping up daytime television sofas and, before long, hosting her own TV specials, no doubt. Oh yes, don't forget the book. Which I'm sure will be appearing soon at a bookshop near you. Give me strength!

***

Like all decent, law-abiding Jamaicans, I was disgusted and disappointed to hear of the mindless murder of Constable Crystal Thomas on 14 July (2015). It happened a couple of days after I left Jamaica to return to England, but before I heard about this tragic event, I hadn't wasted any time extolling the virtues of Jamaica to anyone who would listen.

As someone who left Kingston half a century earlier, and much as I loved the country of my birth, I never seemed to be in a hurry to return (apart from a brief visit to bury my grandmother in 1993). Reason being, all I ever heard about Jamaica was negative. Real live police and thieves abounded in the streets. It seemed like guns and ammunition could be found on every corner. Basically, going to Kingston would be taking your life into your hands. The news media did not help, portraying Jamaica as a bad place full of (seriously) bad people. Nonetheless, I could not let this golden age pass without returning, to retrace my childhood steps. So I sprinkled some holy water on my head, pleaded the blood and boarded the flight from Gatwick bound for Norman Manley International. The negative comments did not only come from the folks in England. Even as I landed and was making my way to immigration and baggage reclaim, a woman thinking she was being kind urged me not to speak to 'anybody'. She said as I sounded so English, the moment I opened my mouth I would be mugged. Great! I just wanted to grab my bags and get the next plane out of there.

I was also warned about 'hustlers' at the airport – usually men trying to take my bags and me to goodness-knows-where. With that in mind, I girded my loins and was ready to fight my way through. Surprise, surprise! There were no 'hustlers' in the airport, or outside. It seemed to me that unless you were boarding a plane or getting off one, you weren't allowed in the building. So far, so good. I walked out of the airport – trouble-free – to be greeted by the majestic mountains and the driver sent by Mona Visitors Lodge, where I was staying. The driver was friendly, convivial and very knowledgeable about Kingston. I am feeling good. All anxieties dispelled. Well, that was until about a mile out of the airport he suddenly pulled over and stopped without warning. Sweet Jesus. Help! What's he doing? "I'm going to get you coconut water," he broke into my anxious thoughts. With that, he formally welcomed me back home. Driving along the Palisadoes. Aaah! *My boyfriend name is Silas, he comes from Palisadoes.* 'Member that?'

That was the start of an amazing experience. Whereas I had been counselled that I would find the Jamaican experience slow and people slack, that was not the case. The staff at my lodgings delivered high-quality service and were as professional as any other place I'd stayed at in the world. They could not have been more friendly, accommodating and helpful. This was reflected in every interaction I had, be it at the bank, in the supermarkets, or on the bus. The bus. I was under strict instructions from my family that on no account should I get on a bus. When my cousin, whom I hadn't seen in 25 years, told me we were going somewhere on a bus, I told her I couldn't. I wasn't allowed. Anyway, after much mirth, I did go on a bus with said cousin. The bus experience was so good I did it again, on my own, from Mountain View to Half Way Tree and then to Mona, on the way striking up bus-stop conversations. I felt all grown-up. There in Half Way Tree I mingled unafraid, with shoppers and street vendors alike, while tucking into my juicy patty, washed down with a can of ginger beer. Sitting in the Nelson Mandela Park, a man called out to me, *"Beg you a drink nuh!"*

I have to say that when I regaled my family in London with stories of my expeditions, they were not best pleased to learn that I was left unattended to walk freely in Kingston streets! But what fun I had. And nobody bothered me. If I had followed people's advice, I would never have left the confines of the UWI campus unaccompanied.

Retracing my childhood steps, I went to Hope Gardens, still magical after all these years, and the entrance to the zoo, with its koi carp pond and waterfall; new to me, and a real gem. Emancipation Park is a dream of a place which came into being long after I left the island. As for Strawberry Hill, a place apart! I can't tell you how many times I found myself asking if I was really in Jamaica.

I was invited to lunch at the delightful Devon House where we tucked into exquisitely presented steamed bammy and breadfruit teamed with authentic curry goat. You can't get that sort of thing in England. Soon after we met, my cousin gave me a bag of mangoes. With all these mangoes I had every good intention of taking some back to friends and family in England. Sad to say, I ate them all in about two days, one after the other. *All a dem!*

And, by a strange happenstance, I stumbled upon a radio station which literally dragged me off the street (well, it's a long story, suffice it to say, I had been to the bathroom on their premises) for an interview about my time spent in England and how my return was going. Yes, man!

As I work in the legal profession, I was keen to see how 'Jamaican Justice' is dispensed so I spent a day in the Supreme Court. I was extremely impressed. The court conducted its matters with diligence and professionalism.

I even had time to take in a performance by *L'Acadco* at the Philip Sherlock theatre, UWI, Mona Campus – classical. Singing the National Anthem for the first time in 50 years at Rollington Town Primary School was a teary-eyed moment.

However, I am keeping it real. I am not blind to the fact that Jamaica has its problems. I think more could be done to fix up Downtown Kingston, and after my day spent in court where the dock was full to bursting with young men on murder charges, and whose mindset was probably no different from the man who killed Constable Crystal Thomas, I couldn't help feeling more could be done to help young Jamaican men.

While the motorway takes travellers from Kingston to places like Manchester and beyond, my sandals nearly came apart walking through some of the potholes in Downtown Kingston and some places in St Elizabeth.

There are so many more wonderful things to see and do, like paying a visit to the National Gallery or devouring sweet fish in Port Royal, so as Arnold Schwarzenegger stated, "I'll be back," or as we Jamaicans would say, "*Soon come.*"

***

This woman, right, went into a supermarket to get some groceries. When she returned to her car, she found her keys locked inside. She prayed and asked God to send her some help.

Within five minutes an old motorcycle pulled up, driven by a bearded man who was wearing an old biker skull rag. He got off his cycle and asked if he could help.

"Yes, I've locked my keys in my car. Please, can you help me?"

"Sure." He asked her to turn away for a second and in that time the car door was open.

She hugged the man and through tears said, "Thank you, God, for sending me such a very nice man."

The man heard her little prayer and replied, "Lady, I am not a nice man. I just got out of prison. I was in for car theft."

The woman hugged the man again, sobbing, "Oh, thank you, God! You even sent me a professional!"

I recently read an article in which a well-known female journalist admitted that women pilots make her nervous. She went on to say that, "Sometimes in life, it feels better to have a strong man in charge." If you could see me now you would see fire coming out of my ears and other extremities! *Like macca jook me!* Brute force is not a prerequisite to pilot a plane safely. It is cool, clear thinking and the ability to handle any situation in the air that is required, not muscles. There is nothing wrong with female pilots. I can vouch for them. Many years ago, I went to Jamaica for my gran's funeral. I flew into Montego Bay via Tampa, at short notice, as there were no direct flights from London to Kingston. Then I had to take an internal flight from Mo'Bay to Tinson Pen in Kingston. The flight was terrible. And to this day it still remains my worst. And it was a man at the helm. With all the dipping and diving he was doing, I thought I was going to die. And me on my way to a funeral already! I was glad to land in Tinson Pen and I spent the whole week in Kingston fretting about going back that way to Mo'Bay. If I'd had the means I would have gone by road. But instead I had to fly back, and what a sweet experience that was. Everything about the flight was smooth and easy and when we ran into a little turbs, the person at the controls knew exactly what to do to give us a safe landing. That person was a woman. God bless her!

***

I don't know about you but I get really annoyed when I see parents wheeling their loco's (otherwise known as a pram with a child seated in it who displays no apparent mobility impediment) on to buses and taking up valuable space which a wheelchair user could well do with. I don't know what it is with these modern-day mums who board buses with their sense of entitlement. In my day, kids were made to get out of their buggies while the buggies were folded up and carried on to public transport. The law has tried to intervene in this in giving access rights to wheelchair users, but on a day-to-day-basis it seems to be powerless and the end result is that many wheelchair users are left stranded at bus stops unable to board a bus. Bus drivers need to be more proactive in implementing the law as it stands, rather than turning a blind eye as they often do.

***

I think I've missed a trick here. I keep in good shape. Watch what I eat and how I eat it. Behave myself and don't cause anybody any trouble. And what recompense do I get for that, eh? But now I hear that the somewhat cash-strapped, and in crisis, National Health Service is thinking about giving free bikes and supermarket vouchers to fat families. I could do with a free bike. In fact, I have wanted to get a bike for years, but I can't afford the hundreds of pounds they go for. But if I were fat and feckless, chances are I could get my porky paws on a good five-gear article that I could ride up and down hills and dales to my heart's content. It's not easy resisting temptation: those lemon drizzle cakes and cheese and onion crisps. It's hard, but I try.

And then I hear that a leading car company is giving car owners up to seven grand to scrap their old motor. When I lived up in the north country, I bought a second-hand car from a roadside car shop. It had a shiny red body complete with black roofing. Pretty little thing. It just didn't go anywhere in particular. The day after I bought it, I drove it to a funeral. I noticed it was moving more slowly than any living car should. But then I was in the funeral cortege and I thought what a clever little car; it just synchronized its little self with the mood. But away from the funeral it still moved very slowly. Long story short. Took it back to the car man who wasn't interested in anything I had to say and basically left me with a 'not going anywhere in particular' car. The car continued to be a right pain in the you-know-what. I tried to sell it, tried to give it away. Nobody would take it off my hands. In desperation, I even tried to get it stolen. Nothing criminal, I just left it on open land unlocked with the keys inside the ignition. And every day when I returned from work I would peek around the corner not expecting to see it, but there it was. I couldn't even get it stolen! No justice in this world.

THE SHORT ARM OF THE LAW

As schoolboy William Cornick is sentenced to life imprisonment for killing his teacher, Ann Maguire, I wonder if this tragedy could have been averted. I think so. Chief Superintendent Paul Money of West Yorkshire police said, "No person acting in authority could have reasonably foreseen the events" of April 28 (2014). I don't agree with his assertion. This was no spur-of-the-moment madness. It was premeditated, and the boy had made his deadly intentions clearly known. It was common knowledge in the school community that he had a grudge against Mrs Maguire and that he planned, at the very least, to do her significant harm. Yet when he turned up at school with knives on that fateful day he was not taken seriously. What did they think he was going to do with those knives? To say that nobody could have foreseen what would happen is ludicrous. An angry boy bearing a grudge, armed with knives, spells trouble. Very serious trouble. That boy should have been searched every time he set foot on school premises and should have been monitored more closely. Never mind about his human rights, he forfeited those when he decided to take a life. Let this tragedy be a lesson to other schools that if they have a pupil who threatens to kill or cause grievous harm to staff or pupils, they should deal with them. Seriously.

***

I have a thing about miscarriages of justice. I don't like it that innocent people are convicted and jailed for a crime they did not commit. However, for years we have had a system that will financially compensate those who unfortunately found themselves in such a bind. For those wrongly convicted of a serious crime, who have spent a lifetime behind bars, losing out on having a family, a career, a life, I don't think any amount of money could compensate. However, as money is the only compensation of substance the state can give, it is not to be sniffed at, and would go a long way to assist them as they leave prison penniless. Now it seems all that is to change. This is because the only way those wrongly convicted can expect to get any compensation is if someone else is found guilty of the crime they were accused of, says the Ministry of Justice. I don't like the sound of this. Here's my point. If the state knows that if they get it wrong it will cost them dearly, they will make more effort to get it right in the first place. But if they have some sort of a get-out clause, that is, if they get it wrong they don't have to pay out anyway, I do believe this would lead to even more miscarriages of justice. How is that progress? I think such a move will impact negatively, especially on black men, where I feel the law weighs heavily against them. Take the case of Winston Silcott. Back in 1987, he was convicted of the murder of PC Keith Blakelock during the Broadwater Farm riot of 1985. He was nowhere near the scene of the crime. His conviction was quashed in 1991 after scientific techniques suggested evidence had been tampered with by detectives. To coin a vernacular, he was stitched-up like a kipper by coppers. For his trouble, Silcott received £17,000 for wrongful conviction and a further £50,000 from the Metropolitan Police. Since then, another man, Nicky Jacobs, was tried and later acquitted for PC Blakelock's murder. So, if a similar fiasco was to take place under the new rules, innocent people could spend years behind bars and not get so much as a biscuit. Pressure needs to be put on the Ministry of Justice to re-think.

***

Here's a question for you. Is the right to protest more powerful than the right to freedom of artistic expression? Don't know? Think about it. I did not get to see Exhibit B. I didn't get time. It was closed down before it really began. The exhibition, a live art installation which was briefly at the Barbican in London in the autumn of 2014, was a critique of the 'human zoos' that showed Africans as objects of scientific curiosity through the 19th and early 20th centuries. Chained motionless, performers were placed in settings drawn from real life. The scenes collectively confronted colonial atrocities committed in Africa, and European notions of racial supremacy and the plight of immigrants today. As spectators walked past the exhibits one-by-one, to the sound of lamentations sung live by a Namibian choir, a human gaze was unexpectedly returned. The exhibition was said to be 'unbearable and essential' and an 'important and provocative work'. Yet it was closed prematurely because protesters –

black people – objected to its use of chained black actors in cages. The thing about that, for me, is that the exhibition expressed what we know as a fact and, equally for me, was telling the truth of past atrocities. I don't see anything wrong with that kind of freedom of artistic expression, nor in telling the truth. In the same vein, Trevor Phillips has recently been described by some as the 'Bravest Man in the Universe'. And what has he done to earn this moniker? He spoke the truth. The truth that dare not speak its name. The truth about racism. People are afraid to talk about it. Afraid to confront it. I agree with Mr Phillips when he says people must be free to say what they want without fear of being accused of racism. If we do not confront it, how can things change? Believe me, we need change. Big time.

We have all noticed it. The closure of local police stations, fewer bobbies on the beat, and now we are being told that the police won't be dealing with certain matters that we have come to expect them to deal with, like going after people who have driven off without paying for their fuel. That's theft. The police say they can't afford to follow up and act on these crimes because they have neither the manpower nor the money to do so. Many years ago, I called the police to report a criminal damage matter and they told me that, if they found the time, they would 'swing by' to see me. To quote pop diva Diana Ross, I'm still waiting for them to 'swing by'. Oddly enough, and far beyond my comprehension, the Metropolitan Police managed to find time to show up at St George's

Primary School in south London after the head-teacher, Geraldine Shackleton, called them on a nine-year-old boy. What criminal act had he committed? Well, none really. Except the poor child, Kyron Bradley, was 'brandishing' a ruler as a sword during a game of 'knights and dragons' with his friends. What did she call them for? Notwithstanding the fact that a child under the age of 10 is legally deemed not to be capable of committing a criminal offence, the police still came. There are a lot of serious crimes that need solving and I think the Met would find their time better spent on solving some of these than traipsing around to a primary school to deal with playground games.

***

A woman and her two young children go missing. OK, bad enough. It takes the police three weeks to find them. Buried in the back garden of their home. Why did it take three weeks? It's not as if the bodies were dumped in a swamp or river miles and miles away from their home in Kent. They were buried in their own backyard. Now, I don't want to be a stirrer, but could it be because the victims involved were, erm… black? Well, how else can you explain it? We are talking about the murders of the former *Eastenders* actress Sian Blake and her children. The actress, who played Frankie Pierre in the BBC soap in the mid-nineties, was last seen on December 13 when she visited relatives in Leytonstone. The inability of the police to get on top of this wasted so much time that they gave the main suspect in the case, her partner Arthur Simpson-Kent, the opportunity to make a run for it. Compare this to another *Eastenders* actress who went missing in 2012, whose body parts sadly turned up all over London, it seemed. It didn't take long for the cops to collar the culprit, who happened to be her brother, who is now in jail for her murder. People are not happy that the disappearance of Ms Blake and her children was not treated as a matter of urgency, particularly as she was a vulnerable person, being in the final stages of motor neurone disease. It does make you wonder what the police consider 'high priority' in terms of missing persons.

∗∗∗

After all the brouhaha over the Bill Cosby sexual assault allegations and accusations that date back decades, he has finally been arrested and charged with at least one of them, for allegedly drugging and sexually assaulting Andrea Constand, a former Temple University employee, at his Pennsylvania mansion block back in January 2004. This arrest came 12 years after the alleged assault. And just within the 12-year statute of limitations in US law in relation to sexual assaults. Obviously, Mr Cosby, who was known for decades as 'America's Dad' and is the brains behind one of the most influential and successful sitcoms of all time, *The Cosby Show*, denies any wrongdoing and claims that whatever relations took place between him and his accusers were consensual. On the other hand, he has admitted in a previous statement that he gave sedatives and hypnotic medication to women he wanted to have sex with. Why would he do that if the women had consented and were willing to sleep with him? And is he suggesting that his 50-plus accusers, who presumably did not know each other, all conspired to ruin the reputation of a most cherished black man, both in the US and around the world? I saw 78-year-old Cosby on the news and he looked frail and weak as he stumbled into court. Guilty or not of these alleged offences, it's time to put this matter to rest once and for all.

NB In April 2018 Bill Cosby was convicted of sexual assault against Andrea Constand. He is awaiting sentencing.

***

Talk about going from the ridiculous to the sublime. A Croydon man was recently arrested by Croydon police on suspicion of 'inciting racial hatred'. In the aftermath of the Brussels terrorist atrocities in March, Matthew Doyle confronted a Muslim woman, who was going about her business in Croydon, and asked her to "explain Brussels". The poor woman, mystified no doubt, replied that it had nothing to do with her. By all accounts, after that bizarre encounter, the two went their separate ways. That would have been the end of the matter but for the fact that Mr Doyle decided this was something he had to share with the population of Twitter. So, he put it out there and, as a result, was charged with inciting (or intending to incite) racial hatred online. Inciting racial hatred is, of course, a crime and a serious one at that; it can be tried in the Crown Court. People have been convicted and sent to prison for it. The most recent case was last December when 22-year-old Joshua Bonehill-Paine was convicted and jailed for more than three years for inciting racial hatred against Jews by distributing images online relating to an 'anti-Jewification' event which was due to be held in

Golders Green, the heart of one of London's largest Jewish communities.

Nonetheless, by confronting this innocent woman Mr Doyle was, to my mind, ignorant and putting it on Twitter makes him at best an idiot full of his own flatulence. But seriously, did he really commit a crime? Based on the spirit and even the letter of the law, I don't think so. I am astounded at how these hard-pressed, hard-up police people can find precious time and resources to spend on some ignoramus; whereas, exactly a year ago, two police sergeants in Croydon allegedly stopped police officers from going to a stabbing incident which was happening very close to their police station. They claimed they had other things to do. Like what? The man died at the scene and his family believes he could probably have been saved had the officers attended. A word to the wise – think on.

I've chanced upon a quick way women can make a fast buck. Sorry guys. It's legal, based on a recent case, and may even be tax-free. All she has to do is get pregnant by a policeman (make sure he is working undercover, though) and whoopee! Set for life. What's not to like? The Metropolitan Police saw fit to pay a woman the handsome sum of £425,000 after she had a baby boy with a man she didn't know was an undercover police officer. When she discovered by chance, some 24 years later, that the father of her son was an undercover cop she was profoundly traumatised. And for that, she was given this huge sum as compensation. The woman, known as Jacqui, was an animal rights activist. Former Special Branch detective Bob

Lambert used the pseudonym Bob Robinson and was tasked with infiltrating the Animal Liberation Front in the 1980s and spying on them. During that operation, he had a relationship with the then 22-year-old Jacqui, even though he was already married with children. She gave birth in 1985, but when the boy was two years old, Bob vanished. The woman only discovered her son's father was an undercover policeman in 2012 after he had been outed by other campaigners. She said she had been receiving psychiatric treatment after learning of Bob's (deceiving) role, and that he was married with children. He played his part well and was even with her during 14 hours of labour. And for such deception, she gets nearly half a million pounds. It seems that all she had to do to get that money was have a baby with a man who lied through his teeth! OK ladies, form an orderly queue.

***

The law is an ass. Or so it seems. The latest married celebrity love cheat is using the law to prevent his dirty deeds being made public. So, he goes to the High Court of England and Wales, takes out an injunction to stop the press naming him and his threesome with another couple, creating a sort of 'cheat's charter'. What is it with these people? He wants to have his cake and eat it too. Presumably, he has enjoyed the fun and pleasure of his illicit liaisons but now wants to keep it under wraps. And hiding behind the law is cowardly. The law should not be obliging to the likes of such low-lifes. Instead, what it does is issue a general warning that anyone mentioning the couple anywhere, including on social media, could face prosecution. What the law should be saying to these philanderers is, if you get involved in dirty deeds do not expect me to cover for you. If this Lothario didn't want people to know about his extra-marital sexual activities, then he shouldn't have engaged in them. End of.

The law is an ass [contd.]. It is against the law to use a hand-held mobile phone while driving but you wouldn't think so judging by the number of drivers seen talking, texting and even taking selfies behind the wheel. I see this all the time, and where are the cops when you need them? Out of sight. Despite there being a law against it, the use of mobiles at the wheel has increased, and when it comes to such illegality men are by far the worst offenders, especially those between the ages of 25 and 35. Driving a car is the most dangerous activity most people ever engage in so why do people make it even riskier by using their phones? Because they can get away with it, that's why. The fear of being caught should have been a real deterrent – but who is going to catch them? What we need are more cops on the road, on the lookout for the commission of these crimes. And there's the rub. Police traffic patrol numbers have dropped since 2014. Why the government brought in a law that they cannot police is beyond me, and the only undeniable thing that has resulted from this pantomime is making the law look an ass.

✶✶✶

I think we need some new people at the top of the criminal justice system. Here we have the head of the Crown Prosecution Service and the Director of Public Prosecutions refusing to act against alleged paedophile, 86-year-old Lord Janner. Janner is accused of sexually abusing children of both sexes from the 1960s to the 1980s. Yet the Crown Prosecution Service, in all its wisdom, ruled that there is not enough evidence to charge him with even one of the 22 alleged sexual offences. At the very least he should have been questioned, as in any allegation of sexual crime. In addition, Alison Saunders, Director of Public Prosecutions, elects not to pursue a prosecution against him. What is stopping them from hauling him in front of the courts is that Janner is suffering from Alzheimer's disease. And it is getting worse, apparently. So he is not fit to stand trial. So they say. Yet he is still an active member of the House of Lords, the upper house which makes laws, and he was well in possession of his faculties to put in a claim of more than £100,000 in parliamentary expenses since he was diagnosed with dementia in 2009. And he was still able to send a note of thanks to detectives who dropped the charges against him. That, to me, shows he understood what was going on and was not, and still is not, quite so demented as we are led to believe. It also appears that Lord Janner's barrister at the time when these allegations first saw light of day in 1991, the late venerable George Carman QC, expressed some surprise that his client escaped charges. It is the victims I feel sorry for. No number of criminal convictions could ever repair lives broken by sexual abuse, but at least, if and when perpetrators are brought to justice, it may go some way to bringing closure and comfort to the victims. Let us hope that this is not the end of the matter and that someone with backbone takes hold of this stench of a matter and makes right some awful wrongs.

***

A woman goes to court and asks the judge to stop her neighbours cooking spicy food. No. This is not a joke doing the rounds. This is for real, peeps. Joanna Cridlin claims the pungent chilli food enjoyed by her neighbours in the flat above hers is akin to antisocial behaviour and has left her choking in her sleep. The jury is out on this one.

***

Whilst on jury service a juror asked to be excused because his wife was about to "conceive". The judge replied, "I expect you mean to be 'confined' but, whichever it is, I think you ought to be present."

***

I can't believe these people sometimes. By that, I mean the Home Office and the Criminal Justice System. Let's start with the Home Office. A few weeks ago they sent a missive to Shane Ridge, a 21-year-old, hardworking, law-abiding white man who was born and raised in Britain, saying that he had 'no lawful basis' to be in the United Kingdom, notwithstanding the fact that his maternal grandmother was

British and his mother had settled status in the UK (she was born in Australia) at the time of his birth. The Home Office told him that not only did he not have 'lawful basis' to stay in the UK, but that if he didn't get his little tush (my translation) out of the UK within a matter of days, he would be looking at another place of residence – jail. And consider the case of Brian White, a 21-year-old black Zimbabwean. He was awarded a place at Oxford University to read chemistry. He is facing deportation. Before he takes up his place at Oxford. Born in Zimbabwe, he was adopted by British-born Peter White and his African wife, and when the Whites came to the UK they brought Brian with them. Brian applied to remain so that he could take up his place at Oxford, but permission has not been forthcoming. Yet, at the same time, it's been reported that five foreign criminals a day are being freed onto UK streets when they should have been deported. There are nearly 6000 criminals born abroad living in the UK and due for deportation, with nearly a third of them on the loose for more than five years. These criminals are not your small-time crooks on the make, but include killers, rapists and drug dealers whom the Home Office seems impotent to deport. This makes me laugh – a spokesman for the Home Office said that "those (i.e. criminals) with no right to be in the UK should return home – voluntarily." Oh yeah? As if! These Home Office people need to get a grip and, to quote Spike Lee, "do the right thing" by all of us.

***

I've said this before and it's probably worth repeating. The law really is an ass. There is a law in the UK that someone who is in fear of their life can use 'reasonable force' to protect themselves or someone else. That's all good and well, but the problem here is that no one quite knows for sure what translates as 'reasonable force'. OK, I suppose it means in simple, man-on-the-Clapham-omnibus terms that if a person comes to attack you with a baseball bat, you can't shoot him. Sort of like for like, if you see what I mean. But it's not always so simple. Lately, we have seen an interesting case of a householder stabbing and killing a burglar who was, we understand, armed with a screwdriver. The householder, Richard Osborn-Brooks, was first arrested for the murder of career criminal Henry Vincent, but the Crown Prosecution Service, for once in their life, got something right and decided not to take the matter further. Mr Osborn-Brooks was probably lucky in that regard. But I don't think people in his position, whose lives and property are under threat, should have to rely on luck. By that I mean, the law should be clear. What the law ought to be saying, to burglars particularly, is if you trespass onto somebody's property to rob them and they kill or injure your backside, so be it unto you. And the law will not be on your side. You can't make it any clearer than that.

***

I watch a lot of crime programmes. Real crime ones, not the fictional nonsense that has the police or CSI catching criminals, getting them convicted and locked up in a 50-minute episode. Not *Midsomer Murders,* though. They take two hours. Although I don't particularly care for programmes where some famous person (like Piers Morgan) visits a prison to speak to criminals (and it's usually murderers) about their crimes. I do find it rather disconcerting how *well-freshed* these inmates look. You wouldn't believe that they were supposedly incarcerated for 24 hours in a three-foot cell and only granted one hour of daylight outside. Take the case of one convict. When she was convicted she had spots and lank, greasy hair. For her television appearance (after being locked up for 15 years) her skin is smooth and soft. Greasy, lank hair is replaced by a smart bob, and she's resplendent in full eye make-up and mascara and the obligatory red lipstick to complete the look. Where are they getting this stuff from? I bet they didn't look that good on the outside!

And Now For a Brief Intermission

Let's forget journalism for a moment…

...and do some real writing!

History Will Tell
(The Grocer's Daughter)

I once loved a man
who belonged to another.

But how could I resist.
Even at 65 he still had the figure and carriage
of a young man half his age.
But his grey eyes were tired
with wrinkles at the corner
And his face was that of a man
who had learnt to accept the present
rather than to have hope in the future.
Yes, he had a wife. Elisabeth.
Empress Elisabeth to be correct.
No need for reproach, Connie.
After all, she did 'set' her man on me.
"Keep him occupied," she had said.

So she could tryst with her Rasputin.
I was not the best actress at the Burgtheater for nothing.
I knew how to play my part.
Perhaps a little too well.
In truth I had other admirers, Count Wilczek and
Prince Ferdinand to name but a few;
Which drove the Emperor crazy with jealousy?
But I was unlike the usual fare of court actresses
with their airs and graces and amended accents.
Franz said so himself.

I introduced him to the 'second society'
Of theatre gossip and belly-laughs.
In return my wardrobe grew
And domestic bills and school fees
Were no longer my concern.
For I was the Mother of a young son.
Franz and I shared happy times together.
The morning meals were the best.
And even my mediocre cigars he smoked
After our modest breakfast, always appeared excellent to him.
He would arrive very early, wearing
The local Tyrolese costume of huntsmen.

Leather breeches and thick socks.

Hardly (to be) distinguished from any other elderly Gentleman taking a brisk morning walk.

But there was not a person on the road

Who did not recognize my Emperor. I too was the subject of much gossip

Within Vienna's society.

Was I the Emperor's trusted confidante and friend

Or cheap lover?

They wondered.

And when the Empress returned to Vienna

From her sojourn in Greece in '83, they said

She had come to sort me out! Indeed!

But let's not dwell on that.

History will tell.

Suffice it to say, time spent at my summer home

With His Majesty was recorded in the royal diary

as, 'those unforgettable hours at Frauenstein.'

Top Flight

It was a late and wet autumn evening when I let myself in through the main door to the mansion house in Cumberland Gardens, SW7.

It had been a long journey, fraught with out-of-date timetables and altered bus routes. I was tired, but I still lingered long enough in the hallway to rifle through the post: electric and gas bills and a growing pile of subscribers' magazines all left on the common hall table by Frederick, our postman. I was disappointed that nothing there concerned me. Ignoring yet another out-of-order sign on the lift that has never understood its true purpose, I started up the three flights of stairs to my top-floor flat.

Two young women passed me on the stairs, arms safely wrapped around each other. Although I hadn't met them before, I smiled and nodded a greeting in their direction, but they were too engrossed in their intimate conversation to speak to a thin, pale, middle-aged woman.

Seb, the lanky city trader from number five who I hadn't seen in ages raced past me, taking the steps two at a time and almost knocking me over in the process. He too had no time for me.

On my way up, I caught the sounds of shrieks and boisterous laughter from Mrs Kowalski's five-year-old twins at number nine, desperately trying their best to rid the world of the bad guys. I imagined them dressed in the matching silver and blue He-man attire they received two Christmases ago, swinging their pretend swords high and low while jumping from bed to bed. How I envy them.

Taking the rickety stairs challenged me in more ways than I care to think about. I hauled myself along the narrow, darkened passage with its creaking floorboards, past Old Tom's flat. My footsteps, now dragging, always brought his meagre mongrel to the door, and as I went past I noted the soft, low growl that came from deep within his throat, and the eventual pitiful whine. By the time I reached my own front door, I was decidedly out of breath.

It was a relief to be home, in my beloved little sanctuary. It was my haven from the cold and often aggressive world of staffroom backbiting, key stages and league tables.

It wasn't strictly mine in the true sense of the word. It was rented. But I had lived there for over forty years, since I first started to work at the local primary school. I had no choice but to rent. A single teacher's pay wouldn't have supported a mortgage back then, and by the time my parents left me some money, I didn't care to move. I took the flat because it pleased me. It had high ceilings and uninterrupted views across the open aspect at the back, and I couldn't resist. I knew from that moment that there was nothing on earth that would ever part me from the flat.

Living in a tenement has its advantages: you're never really alone, for one thing. There are drawbacks – like not having a garden: your own personal bit of earth in which to get your hands dirty. I had to settle for a communal garden, which was nothing more than a narrow strip of green at the rear of the house, with box borders running up to the wall that divided it from adjoining properties. Still, I took pride in making the flat my home.

As I let myself in and removed my hood I heard a muffled sound that stopped me dead in my tracks. It sounded as if someone had dropped something. I stood in the hallway, wondering whether there was someone in the flat, but the noises in these old places can be deceiving, and I didn't hear anything else. I was just being silly.

Streetlight adjacent to the front of the building penetrated the darkness and cast a light through the open door of each room: sitting room, bathroom, and the tiny but adequate kitchen. The bedroom door was closed. I started for the bathroom and glanced around the darkened interior. There was no one lurking in there.

Cautiously, I approached the kitchen and inspected the neat Formica surfaces, shining in the half-light. Again, there was no place for intruders to hide. I was being stupid. If I didn't stop indulging this paranoia soon I was going to start believing it.

The lumpy shapes of the sitting room were hard to make out without turning on a light. It was an old-fashioned room, full of old-fashioned furniture including a mahogany bureau that smelt of secrets. The thought crossed my mind that somebody could be hiding there, and I almost thought I saw a movement in the shadows, but of course, I was being foolish.

From where I stood I could see there was no one hiding behind the armchairs or sofa. Taking my courage in both hands, I edged forward and peered behind the door. Nothing!

Let Me Tell You Something

"There's nobody here," I told myself, but I had entertained the idea too long now for it to lie. I hadn't checked my bedroom. As I crept toward the bedroom door I tried to tell myself that I was only going in there to turn the electric blanket on before bed – but that didn't explain why I was creeping on tiptoes, or why my heart felt like it was crawling up my throat. Something was whispering in the base of my mind that someone was in my bedroom. I chastised myself again for my stupidity and was about to fling the door open when suddenly I heard something – the sound of someone breathing heavily. With anger and anxiety mounting together I opened the door and stepped inside.

The bedside light was on. In the bed was a woman. She was about the same age as myself I guessed and was sleeping soundly. Her arm was outstretched, and a hardback book was lying on the floor, its pages squashed. It must have fallen from her hand when she dropped off to sleep – the muffled thud I'd first heard. I looked at the face of the woman. We must have so much in common: both elderly, alone in a big city, living in a small flat at the top of an anonymous house. I felt a little sorry for her, but there was no getting away from it – I was going to have to get rid of her.

I began by picking up the fallen book, smoothing out the pages, closing it and placing it on the coffee table in the neat little sitting room. That would confuse her! I then took my seat in the rocking chair by the window and waited. You see, even though I have been dead a year, those rickety stairs were really the death of me when I fell down them, I just cannot bear to see anyone else renting my flat.

MEN!

Here is a sorry tale of two teachers, Simon Parsons and Stuart Kerner – both men convicted of engaging in sexual activities with their pupils. In Simon Parsons' case, his wife is standing by him even after he's had a five-year relationship with the schoolgirl who produced a baby, stating to the court that, "He is not a monster. He made a massive mistake." He did not skimp on his romantic overtures to the girl. He took her out for meals and away on lavish weekend theatre trips to London. Some mistake! In the wake of all this, he and his wife, according to her testimony, have grown closer. I guess that's because he now has time on his hands as he isn't busy seducing a schoolgirl. On the other hand, the judge in Stuart Kerner's case caused an outcry by suggesting that it was the schoolgirl who groomed *him*. Cases like these two are becoming less rare and I cannot for the life of me understand why seemingly responsible men would risk their careers, not to mention loss of their families, to get involved with a schoolgirl, especially when they know that their actions, if discovered, will invariably end in conviction and a prison term. This inevitability leads to a loss of livelihood and standard of living. I certainly would not be standing by any husband who did that to me.

***

Most people, I imagine, would like to be considered attractive, and a fair few might even want to be regarded as beautiful. Some of these people enter beauty contests to prove just that. But here's a rarity: a contest that seeks to crown the ugliest. True, true. There is somewhere on the planet a Mr Ugly contest and there are people in this world who would kill for such a title. Take the case of Mr Mison Sere, a native of Zimbabwe. He was recently crowned the winner of this dubious title, but not everyone agreed he was the ugliest, including the runner-up, Mr William Masvinu, who claimed that Mr Sere was not a worthy winner as he was not ugly enough and this kicked off a mini-riot. Fighting to be crowned the ugliest? Give me a break!

***

At last some good news about Black Caribbean men. When it comes to housework they are the best, according to a study carried out by the Institute for Social and Economic Research in Oxford. These men leave their Caucasian and Asian brothers standing when it comes to vacuuming, washing and ironing. This is the kind of man every woman wants. And especially if he can cook, too. Eh, Eh! A proper 'domestic god'. Thanks to their historical roots, Caribbean men tend to have a more balanced family structure and are more inclined to the domestics. So says the researchers. Who wants a man going out in the big wide (and wild) world, toiling by the sweat of his brow and bringing home the bacon when he can be getting that stain out of my silk top I dripped gravy on? *Bring him come*, is what I say.

Twice a year, the great and the good from all walks of life are honoured by the Queen with various insignia, like CBEs, OBEs and MBEs. The most deserving is knighted and elevated to 'Sir' and 'Dame' which I have on good account is an honour not to be sniffed at as it can get you a good, no, a very good table in restaurants at short notice – even when they say they are fully booked. Such a title could probably get you upgraded to first class when you have only paid for economy. Not a bad little gig, I would say. And at certain formal occasions, you get to go in and be seated before the commoners. What's not to like? I tell you, when I get mine, trust me, I will be making full use of it. So it is to my discomfiture that I learn that one of our national treasures, Sir Trevor McDonald says, 'knighthoods are worthless." *Say what?* The veteran broadcaster, who was knighted in 1999, let that slip during an interview with President George W. Bush. Come now, Sir Trevor, don't tell me you have not benefitted even in some small way with that little prefix to your name. Tell you what, if you haven't got much use for your knighthood, (I know as a woman it would be a damehood, but you get my meaning) can I buy it off you?

***

Let Me Tell You Something

I love my reality television shows, especially the ones where Americans go online to meet potential spouses from a foreign country. It's crazy. As one father puts it to his daughter, "There are one billion people in America and you had to go and import one." Classic. There are people in this show who are willing to travel halfway across the world, risking their lives in shark-infested oceans, risking malaria and other deadly diseases, only to find themselves on a Caribbean island being served chicken feet as an aperitif (work that one out for yourself!). I do wonder about these people and what drives them to do this. In the latest series, a 50-year-old white American man is hooking up with a 20-year-old black Haitian girl. What do you think either of them is after? (Don't answer that). You mean to tell me that he couldn't find an age-appropriate partner back in the US of A? And what would a young and attractive girl want with some old geezer? But wait, there's more. That same 20-year-old has, in the shadows, what she calls an 'ex' in the form of a 64-year-old white American man. Now, no matter how things bad and times hard, if I had a 20-year-old daughter who was nookying up with a 64-year-old, who is bound to be even older than me, her *madda... hold me back before I clap her in her head!*

LONDON TOWN

This may come as a surprise to many, but London has been named the most desirable place to work in the whole wide world. Who says so? Jamaicans mostly. Yes, Jamaicans like London, for work and, presumably, for rest and play too. One in six people surveyed said they would prefer to work in the nation's capital. I say this may come as a surprise especially because London, being the financial capital of the UK, has long been associated with work-related stress issues, like 'burn-out' and long working hours. On the other hand, London has much to offer in terms of employment benefits, like London weighting for instance. Many years ago, I relocated from the north country to live in London for family reasons. At first, everyone discouraged me from doing this with the usual "people aren't friendly in London", or, "I couldn't live in London, it's too fast." Soon after I arrived, one person even advised me to return to the north as I would not make it in London. Well, I survived the 'unfriendliness' and 'fast living' and made the most of available opportunities and, after being shouted at a couple of times, I learnt to stand on the right of escalators. I wasn't approached to take part in this survey but, had I been, my response would be likewise. But so as not to make the rest of the nation feel left out, the survey also reveals that the UK is the world's second-favourite place to work, just behind the United States of America, but we won't talk about that.

***

I am all for inclusivity. Everybody welcome. But there must be some exception to that there rule. Recently I attended an exhibition at one of London's premier exhibition venues. It was a vegan show. Not just vegetarian, you know, but proper vegan. To my mind, that would exclude anything on display or for sale that would remotely look like or feel like animal flesh. So I was somewhat perturbed (yes, it happens) when I happened upon a stand selling pork sausages. Real fat juicy porkies, to boot! And even plenty on show to sample. I was completely mystified and wondered why the organisers allowed them in and the only thing that came to mind was – money. They say 'money talks' and these porkies had a lot to say, bold as brass as you like.

***

People can't be serious. Yesterday I opened my usual daily newspaper for a good read and a few pages in I saw pictures of a mass of people weeping. I saw grown men and women wiping real tears from their eyes with their 'kerchiefs. In public. In broad daylight. I wondered who of note, unbeknown to me, had kicked the bucket. Emotions were really running high. Looking closely at the pictures and reading the article, I came to realize what the outpouring of sorrow was all about. Big Ben. Not your Cousin Ben, your Uncle Ben or even Grandpa Ben but that Great Westminster Clock. Big Ben hadn't passed away, he was just off to the repairers (well to be accurate it's the structure the clock sits in that is being repaired) and wouldn't be bonging again for another four years. So the people cried. Some people are fussing about why it should take four years to do the repairs. Some things can't be rushed so I'll say, Ben, you take all the time you need to get fixed up and we look forward to you bonging again when you can.

***

Fake doctor in Harley Street. That sounds like a misnomer. Harley, that most prestigious of Streets in a salubrious part of London, where you would find the country's most eminent medical practitioners, has been housing a bush doctor it would seem. Errol (he calls himself doctor) Denton claims to have cured cancer, arthritis, Crohn's disease and the common cold. How come we missed this? Doctors, scientists (and probably Einstein) have been working their socks off to find a cure, at least for the common cold, but have failed to do so. How come this Errol Denton managed to find it? And, more pertinently, how come this is not widely known, and he making a killing out of this? Well, we know about him now, because he's up in court, innit? For fraud, for unfair commercial practice and for 'selling food not of the quality demanded'. Well, the man is into alternative medicine, claiming he can cure people using food as medicine as well as natural herbs. Man, this kind of talk will land you in jail! I'm not averse to the 'alternative'. For instance, all the tea I drink is herb tea. Including my *cerasee tea*. But what I would really like is a cure for the common cold. It's such a bother to me. However, I won't be consulting him for at £650 for an hour's consultation, it would be cheaper to stock up with Lemsip and Kleenex.

∗∗∗

Whenever I cross a major road where I live, I take my life in my hands. It's not that I am careless or anything like that, but the Green Man that lights up to let me cross in peace and safety, his timing is too short. I have to cross over a three-lane carriageway, then another three-lane carriageway, to get to the other side. People like me have to run. To save my life. I have wondered who orchestrated this because it is plain silly. And because of having to break into a dash to avoid being flattened by vehicles, elderly people are being discouraged from going out, which impacts on their staying active, so says a report out now. This also has a bearing on the disabled, and parents with prams. The lights don't give enough time to cross the road and the cars start revving, which makes me even more nervous. I once met a woman at a bus stop who told me she was taking the bus from one stop to the next because she couldn't face crossing that road, for the reasons stated above.

A man was coming out of church one day, and the pastor was standing at the door, as he always is, to shake hands. He grabbed the man by the hand and pulled him aside.

The pastor said to him, "You need to join the Army of the Lord!"

The man replied, "I'm already in the Army of the Lord, pastor."

The pastor questioned, "How come I don't see you except at Christmas and Easter?"

The man whispered back, "I'm in the secret service."

(INTA)RACIAL RELATIONS

I suppose this could only happen in America. Or could it? After a bit of a mix-up at the baby-making lab, a white lesbian gave birth to a biracial child. And she is far from impressed. She is suing the lab for 'wrongful birth', implying she considers black babies defective and she's sorry the child was born. The mother says she is suing because she needs money for the counselling she will have to undergo for raising a black child. Silly woman. Never heard of Halle Berry or Alicia Keys? As for the child, I bet she'll turn out to be a well-adjusted and balanced member of society, knowing she was a much wanted and loved child.

Good sprite! Not only is Lenny Henry an amazing actor and performer, he recently had a stint as guest editor on the *Today* programme and it proved very insightful of him. Namely, that despite the fact that black people, Asians and minority ethnics (BAME) make up 14.3 per cent of the UK's population, the news consistently comes from a white, middle-class, male perspective. In his role as editor, he wanted to explore what the news would look like if it came from a more diverse perspective and, boy, was he in for a shock. He was not at all loved-up by the listening audience. Some even called him a racist. Others said he had a chip on his shoulder. That is so old hat. How is it when black people speak up about racial inequality, they are the ones at fault, the ones with a chip on their shoulder? I wonder if Lenny will be invited back!

✳✳✳

Listen up, people! It's official. Black people are up to seven times more likely to be stopped and searched by the police than white folk. Well, that's hardly news. We have been screaming this for years. But who took any notice of us? Such blatant acts of discrimination were generally denied by police forces up and down the land. Now we have it, straight from the horse's mouth, so to speak. From none other than the police watchdog themselves. That's a turn-up for the books. Furthermore, Home Secretary Theresa May promises to take a firm stance against police officers who misuse their powers and disproportionately target blacks and ethnic minorities. Even the Ugandan-born Archbishop of York, Dr John Sentamu, the second-most senior person in the Church of England, recently revealed he has been stopped and searched at least eight times, and look how famous he is! Who in Britain doesn't know him? In her recent Stephen Lawrence Charitable Trust Criminal Justice Lecture, Ms May made it very clear to the conference that, if the numbers of stops and searches of black people do not fall, and if stop-to-arrest ratios do not improve voluntarily, as she expects them to, she will 'make it happen' by imposing legal restrictions on the police. That's all good and well and many would say it has been a long time coming, but last year she tried to curb police powers through the law, only to have the attempt slapped down by the Prime Minister's Office. However, no one can fail to notice that we are in election year, so let's hope that this ardent promise from Home Secretary May is not just an electioneering sound-bite to win over voters and, in particular, to garner the black vote; but that the changes she proposes will indeed become a reality and we all can look forward to living and moving about freely in our respective communities without being assiduously and unnecessarily hassled by the police.

***

Racial discrimination is a serious matter. It can stop you getting the job you want and can even prevent you from keeping the job you already have. It can affect the way you are treated by law enforcement and might even have some bearing on which higher seat of learning opens its doors to you. So serious is it that there is even a law against it. Being subjected to racial discrimination is no joke. So it bothers me somewhat when a person, and in this case a young woman who goes by the name of Poppy Smart, calls in the cops to investigate a matter of wolf-whistling. Furthermore, she says, "it's akin to racial discrimination." Is she joking me? She is a 23-year-old white woman. What does she know about racial discrimination? Listen here, Miss Smart. When you reach that mature age when gravity relocates your body parts to the region of your knees, you may well long for anybody to notice you, let alone wolf-whistle at you. In the meantime, please do not equate or confuse your small stuff with the serious matter of racial discrimination.

I am no football pundit, but I have my fondness for the 'beautiful game'. As far as I am concerned football is the easiest of games to understand. You have two teams and two nets, one on either side of the pitch, and whichever team gets the most balls in the opposing net wins. Simple. But the 'beautiful game' has a not-quite-so beautiful problem. Racism. Racism is alive and kicking and, in this day and age, even the Kick It Out campaign is struggling to erase it. It would appear that the Football Association (FA) is not competent to deal with it, and this has frustrated leading Kick It Out campaigner, Troy Townsend. Mr Townsend, father of Andros, a star player for England and Spurs, alleged that three players from his Redbridge Under-17 team were racially abused by way of monkey taunts and gestures from parents of their opponents, AFC Hornchurch, during a recent game. Mr Townsend took his allegations to the FA, who amazingly found that these three youngsters were not racially abused. What, I ask the FA, constitutes racial abuse to them? Their mad decision only serves to compound racism in the game. C'mon the FA, get some balls. Kick racists and racism where it hurts. Give them the boot. Kick them into touch.

I don't know what to make of this. This story that for a decade or more a blonde, blue-eyed woman who goes under the name of Rachel Dolezal managed to pass herself off as an African-American woman; and so convincing was she, she even rose to be president of the Spokane, Washington, branch of the National Association of the Advancement of Coloured People (NAACP). You mean to tell me that in all that time she managed to fool that many people? OK, so she didn't show up to meetings (and go on marches) looking blonde and blue-eyed. No. She turned up heavily tanned and wearing a dubious looking wig of colour. This behaviour opens up a whole can of worms. Firstly, is she taking the mickey out of black people? Was she trying to show how naïve and gullible black people can be? While white people are not barred from being members of NAACP, and some have risen to high positions within the organisation, they declared up-front that they were white. Unlike the deceitful Dolezal. On the other hand, I wonder if we are dealing with other, deeper issues here. Ms Dolezal's parents are white. They say their daughter is white and cannot for the life of them understand why she goes around telling people she is black or even part-black. Such allegations would, of course, cast aspersions on either of her parents. When asked by reporters if her father was African-American, Ms Dolezal said she didn't know what they were implying. Well, for her to be passing herself off as black, or even half-black, what is *she* implying? I wonder if she would still own up to being African-American if she was constantly stopped by the police. Just a thought.

Can you Adam and Eve it? A white singer has been named 'Reggae Artiste of the Year' for 2015. And this singer is none other than our own [British] Joss Stone. When *Billboard Magazine* named her as such, unsurprisingly it unleashed considerable anger among local fans and reggae's supporters around the world. Many of whom took to social media to vent their outrage at the decision, some calling it an insult to reggae veterans and legends. Ms Stone beat off Bob Marley and the Wailers, *(weh you ah seh?)* who came in second place for the award. *Billboard* noted that the 'Artiste of the Year' title is based on record album sales during the year and that Stone's album *Water for Your Soul* had the highest sales figures for 2015 in the reggae genre. Well, that's all right then!

✷✷✷

And speaking of the King of Reggae, a town in northern Italy plans to sell ganja ice cream, which they say is inspired by Bob Marley. Alassio is a resort town covering about seven square miles and has a population of about 11,000. Partnering with Canapa Ligura, which is known for bringing awareness of the health benefits of hemp, the ice cream is created as a tribute to Mr Marley. The ice cream made from hemp seeds is rich in the omegas. This special edition features banana ice cream with caramel, cookie swirls and chocolate peace signs. Don't y'all rush off to Alassio now.

✷✷✷

It may be deep mid-winter, but things are hotting up and it's all kicking off about racism. Racism at the Oscars, racism in the courts, racism at Oxford University; primary school teachers labelling ten pupils a week 'racist', a mother threatening to sue a teacher who called her son 'monkey' in front of a class. I don't know where to start. OK, let us start with probably the most serious one. Racism in the courts. Is there a racial bias in the justice system? Prime Minister David Cameron thinks there might be. And to that end, he asked Labour MP David Lammy to lead a review into the issue. And not only in the justice system, but it's come to Mr Cameron's attention that institutional racism is still with us, alive and kicking. This is sad. That in 2016 we are still dealing with institutional racism. Has nothing been learnt from the death of Stephen Lawrence and all the reviews that took place in the wake of that tragedy? It does not surprise me that there might be racism in the justice system, even at the basic level. A few years ago, I was on jury service at the Old Bailey, London's – if not the world's – most famous and iconic criminal court. And what happened to me? I was the subject of racism. And that was before I even set foot in the building proper. For anyone who has never been to the Old Bailey for any reason, there is only one entrance to the building. Therein enters the accused, the lawyers who will plead their case and the jury who will try them. On entering, everyone must show their ID. About the third day, I noticed that the white jurors were not asked for ID but when it came to me, the security guard asked for mine. A clear case of racism, I would say. So I reported him. And he was dealt with. And every time he saw me after that he gave me dirty looks. If institutional racism still persists in our courts and within the criminal justice system, it needs to be rooted out and dealt with once and for all. Hopefully, we will not need to have yet another review about the state of our institutions in another ten years.

Now, to another type of bias and perceived racism. The Oscars. Not one black actor has been nominated for any of the top gongs. Same as last year. This is not a matter of life and death, I know, I know, but this is clearly outrageous. And it's not that there was a shortage of talent to choose from. There's Michael B. Jordan for his performance in *Creed*, Sanaa Lathan for her performance in *The Perfect Guy*, and Idris Elba for his performance in *Beasts of No Nation*. The fallout from this has movie royalty Spike Lee, and Will and Jada Pinkett-Smith boycotting this month's ceremony. And this apparent snub and lack of diversity among Oscar winners even gets the attention of President Obama who says, "when everybody's story is told, then that makes for better art." True, true. Equally, that [Hollywood] "should provide opportunity for everybody." Well said indeed, Mr President. What's more, the president of the Oscars is African-American. Ms Cheryl Boone Issacs. Well, if she can't make it happen, then who can?

But that's across the pond. Closer to home we have a not too dissimilar problem. So bad, in fact, that it took our beloved Idris Elba to have a not-so-quiet word with Parliament, telling them that, as we live in a diverse Britain, there needs to be more diversity on our television screens. Black British actors, it seems, are at risk of being an endangered species. Such was the concern around this issue that in 2014, Mr Elba and Sir Lenny Henry and others wrote a letter to broadcasters calling for money to be ring-fenced for BAME programmes. Two years on, and very little sign of progress.

Let Me Tell You Something

***

Last month in this column I said a word or two about racism in high places. This, as one might expect, caused our esteemed Prime Minister some concern. So much so, he has ordered various reviews into whether or not such racism claims are founded in our great British institutions. Since writing that piece it has come to my attention, by way of Labour MP for Brent Central, Dawn Butler, that racism is rife in the Big House. Houses of Parliament, that is. She recently gave disturbing accounts on BBC Radio 5 Live of her experience in the House of Commons as a black parliamentarian. In one account, she used the Members' lift and was told by one haughty white male Member that the cleaners' lift was elsewhere. Cheek of it! Nothing wrong with being a cleaner earning an honest day's crust. But why did he assume she was a cleaner anyway? Did she have a mop and bucket upon her person? I imagine Ms Butler was smartly dressed, as she usually is, and probably carrying a briefcase or papers, ready to do business in the House on behalf of her constituents. This pompous nobody didn't have to say anything at all like that to her and I'm sure the 'cleaner' would soon find her way around to her proper lift. He really just said it to make a point, didn't he: that he can say whatever and get away with it. So, Mr 'call me Dave' Cameron, it might be an idea not just to clean up racism 'out there', but to apply some elbow grease to scrubbing up your own House. Then we might have some faith in the laws you make to combat racism in our society.

***

But here's a funny tale. In China, it's great to be black! Black people are well loved-up over there. Treated as rock stars and not like the humble... ahem, cleaner. The Chinese can't get enough of us and black tourists find themselves in an enviable position of being hounded in the streets by locals. They love the black skin. As singer and performer, Anjelo Disons found to his favour. In a video that has since gone viral, he says, "Me and my boys just be sitting here chilling, just sitting – and look at the attraction we've got." We could do with some of that back here, couldn't we? Hmm...

March is the month for women. Mothers' Day [in Britain] is celebrated this month of course, as is International Women's Day, which got me thinking about us black women and how we stand in society today. A report set to be published ahead of International Women's Day states that there is a great pay gap between men and women that leaves women £300,000 worse off during their working lives. This is bad news for the Equal Pay Act which was introduced four decades ago. But what of black women in all of this? Being black and female generally means working twice as hard to achieve success in the business world. And those like Cecila Anam, President of the Royal College of Nursing; Sharon White, OFCOM chief executive; and Karen Blackett, Media-Com chief executive, who have scaled it to the top are few and far between.

And in terms of media representation, which includes the fashion industry, how many black faces do we see adorning those – expensive – glossies? Not a lot. And why is that? Is it that the publishers don't think their magazines would sell if they did not have a lily-white face on their front cover? Thinking ahead, what's the message going out to young black girls? That they are not beautiful enough, that their ethnic nose and full lips are not acceptable? Recently a black model's naturally large lips received hate comments on Instagram yet, at the same time, women like Angelina Jolie is praised for her big lips. The things that make us black women: our big lips, or big butts, or kinky hair are singled out as the main factors that we must change about ourselves in order to be more attractive, in order to be more acceptable. It is true that some black women are praised universally, like Halle Berry, the only black woman to win a Best Actress Oscar, and Beyoncé. Women with light features and button noses. While dark-skinned women like the Oscar's Best Supporting Actress, Lupito Nyong'o, and model Alek Wek are regarded as novelties. And television does not fare any better either. Here is a question for you. Who is the top black female star on British television? In anything? Yes, I know, her name escapes you.

But while you are still scratching your head, I think there is something smelly going on in the TV programme, *Doctors*. I love *Doctors*. That mid-afternoon, suburban soap that is so good but generally gets overlooked because of its afternoon slot. In *Doctors,* there was a character called Mrs Tembe, brilliantly played by Lorna Laidlaw. Mrs Tembe first appeared in the programme in January 2011 and departed in February 2016, having, it seemed to me, been pushed out by what I believe to be racism by the new practice manager. I thought, here's a chance for the BBC to develop this story and move it into a satisfactory conclusion, whereby racism is not tolerated in the workplace. But all we see is Mrs Tembe being forced to leave the job she loves and nothing done about her antagonist, a powerful white male. Art imitating life? I wonder.

✳✳✳

And staying with International Women's Day, I think it would be nice to remember a certain woman who was quite instrumental in bringing about changes that affected women in the 1970s. She probably isn't that well known throughout the UK, but she certainly made her mark in Brixton, south London. I speak of none other than Jamaican-born Olive Morris who, even in her short life, was a fearless campaigner for women and their rights. She was a founding member of the Organisation of Women of African and Asian Descent (OWAAD) in London, established the Brixton Black Women's Group, was a member of the British Black Panthers movement, and helped found the Manchester Black Women's Cooperative and Manchester Black Women's Mutual Aid Group. Let's hear it for Olive.

✳✳✳

Radio was my first love. And I have loved listening to it ever since I was a small child in Jamaica. I would sit around the Radiofusion, suitably placed on the dining table, listening to everything from the Maytals to the obituaries. And when my father bought me my own transistor radio that barely fit into my palm, I was in radio heaven, listening to the glorious *Life in Hopeful Village* in a little corner all by myself. Fast forward a lot of years and living in the UK. I still love the radio. Love to listen to it and be on it. I had a little stint on BBC Radio Manchester back in the 1980s. And since then I have presented and produced my own shows, even winning a few little prizes along the way. Yeah! In terms of listening to local radio, I may well be in the minority, in every sense of the word. A recent review by BBC's own watchdog says that BBC local radio 'is much too white' and is failing non-white audiences. That is, when it comes to their own local radio, Black, Asian and other ethnic minority groups are not tuning in. Why is that, I wonder? Could it be because local radio presenters are mostly white? I did a little research of my own and, indeed, that seems to be the case. The BBC themselves say that's not good enough and that they are making every effort to increase diversity on air. Listen, Mr Man at the BBC, if you need to make your numbers up, I have form. I can do it. Check me.

✳✳✳

When a black Oxford University student bragged on Facebook that he had reduced a white waitress to tears when he and his friend refused to tip her after she served them, he thought he was being smart. But he was the one looking like a blockhead after sympathisers raised thousands of pounds for her on an online fundraising page. Ntokozo Qwabe, who is studying law at Oxford, felt he had to make a point about racism whilst dining in a café in the Western Cape of South Africa. He and his friend also gave the waitress a note stating that they would not be tipping until they [white people] 'return the land'. The irony of all this is that he is a Rhodes Scholar, and were it not for this scholarship, instituted and funded by Cecil Rhodes (whose regime in South Africa and Rhodesia was considered to be racist), he would not have found himself at this prestigious seat of learning. Surely, he must have known about Cecil Rhodes and his background and what he stood for. Yet he unashamedly accepted the 'white man's money', this racist white man's money. Isn't that rather hypocritical?

***

One of my favourite films of all time is *Cool Runnings*. You know, the one about the Jamaican bobsleigh team that competed at the 1988 Winter Olympics in Japan. I think the television companies like it too because every now and then it's on TV and that's nice. Anyway, of late there has been a bit of an issue in Aberaeron, a seaside resort in Wales, regarding the film, to the point where coppers were called in to investigate a case of racism. Reason being, in this seaside resort of Aberaeron there is an annual village carnival and on this recent occasion (white) revellers blacked up to look like a comedy Jamaican bobsleigh team. Dreadlock wigs and all. Members of the local Labour Party didn't like this one bit and described these antics as, and I quote, "racism – pure and simple". What you think?

TOO POOR TO BREED

As a British Jamaican, I'm appalled at Cambridge academic George Steiner's negative comments about Jamaicans (Mail). He suggests they're idle and do nothing but breed: show me a modern Jamaican family with six children today. They can't afford it.

On holiday recently, I saw a non-black family who had nine children: my friend and I counted. And — for the record — Jamaicans aren't the only race who play reggae music these days: the genre has been repeatedly plundered by various white musicians.

Mrs J. LOVELOCK,
London NW10
Published in the Daily Mail, September 2008

ALL IN A DAY'S WORK

White Dee[3]: what's all the fuss about? That's what I am asking. As was a TV programme shown on New Year's Day. Big, big New Year's Day, this is the best Channel 5 could offer, a documentary on a very overweight woman idling her life away on benefits. And she is a star! She even had a spot of speaking at a fringe event at the recent Conservative Party Conference. Talking about what exactly? She also earned £1,500 for just one-hour dancing with students during personal appearances at nightspots. If she was fit enough to be jigging it in nightclubs then she was fit enough to work. What kind of country are we that we reward the idle and lazy and big them up on TV? Where is the incentive for putting your back into education or learning a trade and finding worthwhile employment that will enable you to pay your way through life?

---

[3] Deirdre Kelly, known as 'Dee' and sometimes called 'White Dee', appeared in the TV documentary series *Benefits Street* in 2014 and 2015.

A store manager overheard an assistant saying to a customer, "No, ma'am, we haven't had any for some weeks now, and it doesn't look as if we'll be getting any soon."

Alarmed by what was being said, the manager rushed over to the customer who was walking out of the door and said, "That isn't true, ma'am. Of course, we'll have some soon. In fact, we placed an order for it a couple of weeks ago."

Then the manager drew the assistant aside and growled, "Never, never, never, never say we don't have something. If we don't have it, say we ordered it and it's on its way. Now, what was it she wanted?"

The assistant smiled and said… "Rain."

Teachers are supposed to be intelligent. And they usually are. So how come on one fine day the teachers of a primary school in Southampton decided to show Michael Jackson's *Thriller*, certificate 15, to their seven-year-old pupils. Which part of 'certificate 15' did they not understand? I have seen that *Thriller* video with dancing duppies and werewolves and I watched most of it through my fingers. And I'm big. So it comes as no surprise that these poor little 'uns at Berrywood Primary suffered night terrors as a result of watching it. Even though the headmaster apologised to angry parents, I think what this school needs is six of the best.

***

Once upon a time, there lived a young woman who made her bed in Holloway. Prison that is. She was doing porridge for drug smuggling. Six and a half years, in fact. In the dead of night, she heard a ruffling and a shuffling and this she mistook for God answering her incantations because she had been praying. Alas, it was not the Almighty responding, but a big rat that had been rustling around her prison cell. This was a wake-up call if ever there was one and, after serving her time, Gina Moffatt decided to leave the world of criminality behind and walk the path of the straight and narrow. Now, seven years after her release, she is a very successful businesswoman owning a string of profitable businesses, including two cafés selling Caribbean-style food, and a florists, that boast revenue of almost £200,000. She even employs former jailbirds along with other disadvantaged Londoners. The award-winning Ms Moffatt, whose cafés have been visited by royalty, no less, has made every effort to turn her life around, and her remarkable transformation is not only a credit to herself but also an inspiration to others. I hate to say it, but it appears that crime does pay, sometimes.

***

A few years ago I attended a food exhibition at Olympia in London. There were all these fancy stalls in central positions, and stuck in a little back corner, as if a sort of add-on, was a tall dread-locks man who, in his gentle way, was trying to persuade me and my friend to try his homemade sauce. We did, and boy, it was real nice. Imagine my surprise when a few months later reclining on my sofa, watching *Dragons' Den*, I see coming up the stairs, strumming his guitar, singing his song *Reggae, Reggae, Sauce* this same man who was stuck in a little out-of-the-way corner. I sat up. And paid attention. Levi Roots persuaded Peter Jones to get involved in his embryonic enterprise and the rest, as they say, is history. And a rich story at that because according to the Reality (shows) Rich List, Jamaican-born Mr Roots has recently been named as the richest male reality star, with an estimated £30 million fortune. Born in 1958, Levi came into his phenomenal success and great fortune at a mature age, so it's just as well he didn't know that if you haven't made your fortune by age 30, well, you can forget it. So say American researchers who found in a recent study that if you are over 30 and still dream of making your fortune you will be sorely disappointed because it's not going to happen. Tell that to Levi Roots and the likes of him. 'Tis true, you are neither too old, nor have left it too late to realise your dreams. Sweet dreams are made of this.

※※※

Well, kiss me neck! The 'Saturday job' is dead. Shock! Horror! Speaking as a former 'Saturday girl' this is distressing. I started my working life doing a Saturday job at Woolworths when I was in the lower sixth-form. This job not only gave me my own money to spend on essential things but also on frivolities. It also instilled in me the importance of the work ethic. From that early age, it taught me how to work alongside different people, people who were older than myself, people who had extensive experience of the working world, and how to get along with workmates and customers, however challenging. Throughout my time at Woolworths, I worked on

'Cosmetics'. This became the gathering place for us young girls to share gossip, moan about parents, school life and boyfriends. Back in that day, it was commonplace and important for young people to have a Saturday job. According to research, people who combined full-time education and work were more likely to be in employment and training later on and likely to be earning 15 per cent more than those who didn't work. We good people of Britain cannot allow the Saturday job to die. We need to rise up and take action. Long live the Saturday job!

Quote of the Month: "I always wanted to be an accountant." Who said that? Rapper Tinie Tempah. Fancy that!

The headline screamed at me: 'More than 1000 practising doctors have a criminal record', including sexual and child porn offences. And the National Health Service sees fit to let these criminals loose on poor vulnerable and unsuspecting patients? I know times are hard and a lot of medics are leaving the UK to find their fortunes on foreign shores, but when you have a criminal record, especially those involving offences against the person, as these sexual offences are, they are supposed to preclude you from getting, having or even keeping certain jobs. And I would have thought being a doctor, in a position of trust, dealing with the defenceless, would have been one of them. There would appear to be no list of crimes for which a doctor can be struck off and for there to be such a list it would require an Act of Parliament. Bonkers!

※※※

What's in a name? To most people, not a lot; while for others it means a great deal. Take the name of Kayo Anosike. I think this is an agreeable name to be walking around with. It has a nice ring to it. But if it was your name, do you think it would get you a job? Perhaps not. This is the real name of a real woman called Kayo Anosike. And, in keeping it real, she applied for a great many jobs using this, her real name. As you do. But guess what? She didn't get a single job she applied for, including those of the admin kind. Even though she was well educated and well able to do them. You may well wonder why not? In case it has escaped your notice, Kayo Anosike doesn't sound like your typically English name. In fact, it is African. That is why, Ms Anosike believes, she was not getting jobs she applied for. So she decided to try a different tack to *pop dem*. She applied for jobs with a name change, calling herself Kayla Benjamin, a more British-sounding name. And, guess what, she got the first job she applied for. I don't know about you, but I think it is disgusting that she or anyone should have to go to such lengths to get a job. Your name is your name. That's who you are. That's your identity. What is really sad about this story is that Ms Anosike is not alone. She is not the only person who has had to resort to this sort of deception to even get an interview. In a recent survey by Nottx, the blind hiring platform, nearly a quarter of professional women in the

UK have changed their non-white sounding names to traditionally British ones in order to get a job. This survey also reveals that most of this discrimination is found in the finance and IT sectors. Now, I am no Einstein, but why in the world would my name matter in the realm of finance and IT? What my mama and papa named me should have no bearing on whether I can add up or tell my mouse from my moose. What the employer should be concerned about are my skills and ability to do the job, and not my name.

This is funny. The Ministry of Defence (MoD) is being sued for millions of pounds by hundreds of black soldiers. Over what? Well… the cold. The cold? I wouldn't have thought the MoD had any control or sway over the British climate and its workings. I don't understand. Tell me more. It's all a bit outlandish, but stay with me. Black soldiers, particularly those from African countries such as Nigeria and Gambia, are suing the MoD for failing to take into account their ethnicity, that is, them being black. If they had taken that into account, their being black, they would not have sent them to cold countries like Canada or Norway, and they would not have suffered hand and foot cold injuries. That is, their hands and feet getting cold and numb. I am not doubting for a second that these fine men have a case, but what is interesting is that they voluntarily signed up to join the British army from their country of origin. It is not beyond anybody's comprehension that Britain has four seasons. Winter being one of them. Sometimes we get all four in one day. By heck, we even get snow in spring and autumn. My thing is this. If you sign up for the army, you go where they send you. *Dems the rules.* You can't pick and choose. It's not dolly mixtures. What if white soldiers said they didn't want to go to Africa or the Caribbean because '*mi caan tek de heet, maasa. Itta bun mi up*'? What then? I live in the UK and my hands and feet get cold and numb in the winter. Who can I sue?

Strike a light! I hear that electricians are earning about £150,000 a year. That's more than judges and surgeons get. How is it that someone who probably left school with no qualifications, never had to bust a gut or stayed up until the wee small hours completing university assignments, or even trained for a heavy-duty professional exam gets to be worth that much? The job of the Prime Minister doesn't even warrant that pay scale. I have to say though that, in my time, I have had a couple of electricians in my home fixing me lights. They were seriously good-looking, and I wondered why they weren't using their natural talents sashaying down some runway. But they choose to light up (pun definitely intended) our lives with much-needed skills.

FAMILY MATTERS

This is a tragic case. A man and woman were found dead in a hotel swimming pool in Essex. The hotel was fined £200,000 for health and safety breaches even though safety breaches had not led to the couple's deaths, which remain 'unexplained'. The tragedy here is that the man in question was a married man who had taken his mistress to the hotel for a surprise weekend break to celebrate her birthday. Eye-witnesses say the couple seemed to be having a lot of fun splashing about in the pool. I wonder what he told his wife he was doing that weekend?

***

Finding a good man to hook your wagon to can be like trying to find a needle in a haystack. Finding a good, rich one is like trying to find two needles in a haystack. But ladies, hold on to your girdles, help is at hand. Just listen to what your auntie Lara tells you. Dating expert Lady Lara Asprey (she is not exactly titled but this is how she styles herself, and why not?), has come up with what she thinks is a foolproof way to bag a billionaire. And she charges an awful lot for this info. Obviously, I am very interested in this. When I was a little girl, while other girls dreamt of marrying their Prince Charming, I dreamt of marrying a Rich Man. I was just keeping it real. So here we go. Rich men (apparently) don't like trophy wives or arm candy who have been under the knife. I'm well in here. He'll love my under-eye baggies and droopy jaws. And as for the crinkle neck: sorted! Next, they don't like probing questions. So, I won't ask how he made his billions and how soon can we get married and will we be honeymooning on Mustique. This is because they find it refreshing if someone is not interested in money. Their money. And as apparently you can't fake this, I'm off to acting classes. But here's the bit I don't like. I am supposed to have my own dreams, be a goal-digger. What's that to the purpose? My only goal here is to bag him! I must also remember that when we go on dates, I should let him pay for the first two but make some pretence that I want to pay or at least chip in. I am a bit worried about this part. What if when I run joke with him he says "If you insist" to my pretend offer? I'd be in a right pickle then! I used to know a man who was as mean as the devil. A right el cheapo. Over the years we went on a few dates, to dinner and to the theatre. Could I get him to pay for anything? Could I heck. If he had got his way, he would have had me paying for his meals, his theatre outings, his meds... We always ended up having an argument over his bad manners. The thing is, he was a well-educated professional (have to keep schtum about his profession or he'll know I am talking about him) with loads-a-money. In truth, he was rather low rent. So I'll have to seriously think about whether I want to offer to pay. More importantly, rich men like women with sparky characters. In me, they have come to the right place. Ask my friend. Also, Lady Lara's golden rule is, "think tall, hold your head up high, keep your back straight, shoulders back, tummy in and hips forward." Got it. Here we go!

***

Wife to husband: Darling, shall we go upstairs and make love?

Husband: I can't do both.

'Tis the season to be jolly' and I will be, just as soon as I get a few things off my chest. Not so long ago we had something of an outrage about absent fathers, and in particular black absent fathers, who shouldered much blame for the involvement of young black boys in gangs and general criminality. Added to that was a widespread feeling that boys (and girls presumably) brought up without fathers were the scourge of society's ills. Even Prime Minister David Cameron got in on the 'baby-father' debate, urging black fathers to 'be more responsible'. Absent fathers equal single mums, right? And, by all accounts, that spells trouble, right? So I was somewhat bemused to find out that there is a growing trend in white middle-class women using IVF and artificial insemination to deliberately become single mums. Even more shocking, they say fathers are a thing of the past. Hold on one strawberry-picking minute. How is it OK for white women to be lauded and take up many column inches in national newspapers and glossy magazines advancing the case for 'absent fathers', maintaining their child does not need a father. At least in the black community a man was involved, even if it was just to eat and shoot before he leaves. A child would at some point have seen or at least have some knowledge of their father. In this case, 'a lifestyle choice' as one of these test-tube-baby mums puts it, a child would have no idea who the daddy is. It is one thing for a child not to have a father around through tragic circumstances, but quite another to deliberately bring a child into the world without one.

✷✷✷

This is not supposed to be funny, but it is. Picture this. You are at the funeral of your loved one, be it your gran, your granddad or your bezzie mate. You are sitting in the black stretch limo, your heart broken, your weeping eyes peeled on the hearse in front of you bearing your loved one. You do this for nine miles. Only to discover that when you came to the cemetery, the hearse bearing your loved one to its final destination has gone AWOL. This was the experience of a family in Haverford-west, Pembrokeshire, and more akin to a scene straight out of *Only Fools and Horses*. I have to tell you, hearses have a mind of their own. When my gran passed away in Jamaica some years ago and we were following the hearse in the funeral cortege, somehow or other the hearse bearing her to her final resting place gave us the slip. We spent a long time driving around and around some back corners trying to find it and when I stopped to ask some young boys having a kick-about if they had seen a hearse come past, the bemused look on their faces was a picture.

Some people are just downright greedy. Take a certain Mrs Varsha Gohill. She was married to a very rich Mr Gohill and when they divorced she pocketed a cool £10 million. For a great proportion of us women, that's a whole lot of shoes, handbags, leg-waxing and eyelash extensions. But Mrs Gohill claims that's not enough for her to get by on. People, this 50-year-old claims she needs more than £10m to live on. It's my bet she will not live long enough to spend all of that. Not to mention the interest she will accrue on such a substantial sum. Where do these people come from? But here's another side to the marriage business. I know times are hard, but this takes the biscuit. A Kenyan man has offered President Obama 50 cows to marry one of his daughters. The older one. Malia Ann. Hey dude, this is a prezzi's girl we are talking about. A 'First Daughter'. If this is all a 'First Daughter' can fetch, I wonder how much I would go for!

A young woman was taking an afternoon nap. After she woke up, she told her husband, "I just dreamed that you gave me a pearl necklace for Valentine's Day. What do you think it means?"

"You'll know tonight," he said.

That evening, the man came home with a small package and gave it to his wife. Delighted, she opened it — only to find a book entitled 'The Meaning of Dreams'.

I recently heard a story of how a marriage broke up when the wife came home to find her husband giving their baby daughter and their dog a bath together. That's wrong. Apparently, even the dog looked as if he knew it was wrong. A dog is a dog. On no account should a dog be taken as a human being. That is, you don't kiss them on the lips, take them into your bed or share a bath with them. Even though some of them can be cute, experts say dogs can carry diseases that could make you seriously ill or even kill you. I am no dog hater. When I was growing up we had a sweet dog, Blackie. God rest his soul. He was a much-loved, faithful little fellow who would wait for me each evening after work at the T-junction near my home and he would trot proudly alongside me keeping me company. I still think of him with great fondness to this day. But I never lost sight of the fact that he was a dog.

Sorry, it is said, seems to be the hardest word. And if you find yourself in the doghouse because you have offended or upset your partner in some way, read on, because I have a plan. A six-point plan to be precise. First, you grovel, grovel, grovel, grovel and grovel and when you have exhausted yourself with all that grovelling you grovel some more. Seriously though, if you want to be reinstated and take your place in the marital bed you need to firstly take responsibility for the wrongdoing, show that you are remorseful by expressing regret for your actions and, most importantly, repent and beg for forgiveness; and if that doesn't work there is always the tried and trusted. It involves bottom and kisses.

***

Singer Tom Jones (now Sir) had numerous affairs throughout his very long marriage to his wife Linda who recently passed away. He had a two-year relationship with Mary Wilson of the Supremes and also had a very public and well-documented liaison with a former Miss World, Marjorie Wallace. He went on to have another relationship with a Katherine Berkery who bore him a son. And a Miss Charlotte Laws comes forward to state that, as an 18-year-old virgin, he seduced her. And that's just the tip of the iceberg because, by his own admission, Jones had sex with hundreds more women. And in response to all this, Jones's biographer, Robin Eggar, states, "What does matter is that he always comes home." And that makes it OK, does it? These affairs no doubt caused Mrs Jones no end of grief. But she stayed in the marriage. My question is why do women stay with men who put it about like this? A few years ago I was asked to be on a couple of TV talk shows where this subject was under discussion. At the time, the wives of President Bill Clinton and Jeffrey Archer (English peer and author) had come under some fire as to why they chose to remain with their cheating and philandering mates. I don't exactly know the reason why, but my guess is that these women weren't living a humdrum life in a two-up, two-down terrace with an outside toilet. Their men have money and power and oftentimes a title. Women in these circumstances clearly have weighed up the pros and cons and concluded that it is far more tolerable to weep in satin pillows than cotton ones.

Let Me Tell You Something

***

Riddle me this, riddle me that. Guess this parable, or perhaps not! An 86-year-old woman claims she has had "an almost unbelievable shock" when she is faced with proof that her 61-year-old son is not the biological spawn of her husband but that of her married lover. Notwithstanding that this son is the spitting image of that same lover. Notwithstanding the fact that other family members noticed and commented on the striking resemblance. Notwithstanding the fact that the son looks nothing like her then husband. Even so, such discovery has come as a shock to her. Hmmm... Whilst this lady is not the first, and certainly won't be the last, woman to sleep with more than one man at a time and even become pregnant in the process, it does beggar belief that it has taken over sixty years and the intervention of science to tell the truth of who that child's biological father really is. As a child grows, behavioural characteristics of the daddy will emerge as well as physical characteristics. Every mother knows this. And not just the mother. Even the said married lover in this case, could see the resemblance from a distance and believed the child who grew up to be the head of the Anglican Church was his own. Quite frankly, having that DNA confirmation was a waste of everybody's time and money.

***

So much for the "my kids don't need a dad" recitation espoused by a growing number of single, white middle-class women who have taken to having children by artificial means.

Now the chickens have come home to roost. Because these children, who were conceived without a man present, are now asking "where's my dad?" I always believed that having children is not just about yourself, but primarily about that child (or children) you are planning to have and what life you intend to offer them. Whilst we don't live in a perfect world and conception and pregnancy for many women may not have been all mood music and rose-scented candles, the welfare and wellbeing of the child is always paramount. The kids of these so-called 'solo mothers' don't feel quite so happy about their mothers' selfish decision and they have developed mixed or negative feelings about not having a father. Not least because they don't know their biological father nor have the faintest of who he is. That must lead to some identity crises. One of the most difficult things about being a single parent is when you are angry with your children. If you lose it with them they haven't got another parent to turn to. There's no 'bad cop, good cop' here. Still think this is a great idea, you 'solo mums'?

✶✶✶

This can't be right. Middle-class families with children are the new poor. How so? How can you be middle-class and poor at the same time? A bit of an oxymoron there, methinks! It used to be if you were middle-class – that is a doctor, lawyer, college lecturer or similar – you were rich. You lived in a des-res, drove a fancy car that wasn't made in Britain and had to hand a couple of gym memberships. What's happened to all that? Answers on a stamp, please.

Let Me Tell You Something

※※※

Because of television shows like *Who Do You Think You Are?* and the rise in interest in checking one's ancestry and genealogy, I am often asked if I would be interested in finding long-lost or forgotten blood. No thanks! Why would I want to do that? I have enough trouble with the family I know now. Why would I want to pay good money to bring more people into my life to fuss with me? Why? And I don't understand this 'need to know' obsession. What does it matter to anyone, or how will it enhance their lives, if it comes to light that they descend from aristocracy or even royalty? How does that information help with paying the rent on a cramped council flat on a sink estate? You can't take that information to the water or electricity board and hope for a discount, can you? (I have just kissed my teeth right there!)

Mi cum yah fi drink milk, mi nuh cum fi count cow

LET'S GET POLITICAL

It cannot have escaped anyone's notice that we are knee-deep in election fever (May 2015) and by the time you read the next edition of this newspaper there will be another government in office. What shade will they be? Blue, Red, Yellow or even Green? Then there is UKIP. Some of you may ask, "Am I bovvered?" I'm not normally, but we should be, if for no other reason than that under the current Coalition the number of unemployed black and ethnic minority youths increased by 50 per cent. The Labour party states that the official statistics showed that 41,000 black and ethnic minority people aged 18 to 24 have been unemployed for more than 12 months and accuses the Tory party of failing our youths. This is clearly not good. It is a huge waste of the next generation's skills, potential and talent, and in the long run, it will cost our young black and minority ethnic youth, their families, and the economy. Something must change and here's hoping that whatever shade of colour is standing on the steps of No.10 Downing Street on 8 May, they will make every effort to ensure that our young talent does not wither and dry up and fall by the wayside but is at the very least assisted to show the world what greatness they are made of.

***

On a crisp autumn morning, a dreadlocks white man going for his usual morning run found himself in a spot of bother. He met David Cameron, the Prime Minister of this great nation, and he didn't know it. This is a serious matter. Mr Cameron has been Prime Minister for four and a half years. Dean Farley, the unfortunate man, insists he had no idea he had bumped into the PM as he didn't make him out. Never mind being manhandled and cuffed by men in suits and sporting shades for having crashed into the PM, I think he should be escorted to the Tower, pronto. The Prime Minister can be seen on numerous walkabouts up and down the land pressing the flesh; he is constantly in the papers and on the telly, yet there are still some people in this country who don't even know what he looks like. Why go through all that trouble to be leader of your country when your subjects can't tell you from Adam? Might as well the PM had gone about with a paper-bag over his head.

***

I am thinking of going into politics, if only to change a certain section of the law. For too long I have been concerned about a law that protects the identity of rape complainants yet reveals that of the suspect. Even if the suspect is eventually prosecuted and acquitted, the damage to his name and reputation is irreparable. The latest in this type of atrocity, yes, I do use that word purposefully, as what follows amounts to an atrocity, is the case of four young men, Thady Duff, Leo

Mahon, Patrick Foster and James Martin, who have been put through hell having been accused of and taken to court for sexual assault and rape after a drunken sex session involving the complainant. The case collapsed at the door of the court for lack of evidence. Of course, rape allegations should be taken seriously by the legal system and the public but not at the cost of the accused. I do not have a problem with the complainant remaining anonymous, but so should the accused. And if the prosecution fails, then while it would be a sore and bitter experience for those men and their families, at least they would not be publicly named and shamed forever. For the Crown Prosecution Service to bring a case with no sound foundation and no real prospects of a conviction does not do the complainant any favours either. Complainants in sex cases used to be ignored, but recent reforms ensure that their allegations are taken seriously, and codes of practice and changes in court procedure ensure they are more likely to testify at trial. The concern, however, is that the balance has shifted too far, which in effect puts suspects on trial even before they are charged. If this absurdity is allowed to continue unfettered, sooner or later real rape complaints will not be taken seriously by anybody. And where would that leave us? It may be a long time coming but a change in the law has got to come.

***

Well, *blouse and skirt me*. Single mum of eight, Marie Buchan, is in a state of distress. She has to get off her comfortable rear end and get a job. Why? Her very generous welfare benefits of

£26,000 a year are being cut to a "measly £23,000". And she is not happy. "This benefits cap is getting out of control," said she. With that kind of insight, she should run for Parliament. "It is a constant struggle," she wails. Yes, I know what you mean, love. It's a hard life getting twenty-six grand for nothing. She started having kids at 19 and has been on benefits ever since. She states that she has never had a job and you don't need to be a rocket scientist to work out that she probably hasn't done much to contribute to the public purse either. But we have a system that allows this kind of malarkey.

Tap yu noise, mek mi ears namn grass

CHRISTMAS A COME

Let me start off by saying that this country of ours is a Christian country. We respect other faiths. We respect whatever and however people wish to practise their faith and religion, but we are still fundamentally a Christian country and culture and a hallmark of this Christianity is the Lord's Prayer. Now, I have never seen this before but, in this run-up to Christmas 2017, the Church of England produced a film of the Lord's Prayer. Basically, it's an advert encouraging prayer, but big-name cinemas like Odeon, Cineworld and Vue have banned the video from showing at their venues. The company which sells advertising at these cinema chains said the Church of England film could be seen as offensive. Offensive? To whom? Believe me, everybody prays. At some time. When your house is up for repossession and you face being evicted with nowhere to live or your child is late home from school or is sick unto death, you pray. Interestingly, both Christian and Muslim leaders, and even those who claim to be atheist have called this refusal to show the video ridiculous. Unbelievably, these cinemas do not seem to mind showing adverts for alcohol, violent video games, sexualised perfume commercials and the like to young audiences.

***

Christmas is not only coming, it's here. If you've visited some leading department stores, it seems to have been around since September. Christmas is a time for sharing. And caring. But that seems to be all good if you have someone to share and care with. However, if you don't, Christmas can be a very lonely time. One-way loneliness can be overcome is through volunteering. Especially at Christmas time, there are uber-opportunities to help at homeless shelters and visiting and spending time with the elderly and vulnerable. Research published in recent years suggested black people who want to volunteer for charities are often overlooked because voluntary organisations fail to reach out to black and ethnic minority communities. The research also found that even if people wanted to volunteer their time, they did not know where to go or who to ask. So we need to be pro-active. Get out there and find it, because the need is out there. Volunteering is one of the best ways to gain new skills and, for those in-between jobs, it can increase employability as well as helping the local community. I like volunteering and over the past few years, I have volunteered for charities like Crisis at Christmas and met people from all backgrounds. And it's great fun.

***

Now, here is a real Christmas Story. Imagine this. You have gone to your local church for the nativity display and, as is the usual, there are the shepherds, the three wise men from the East and of course Mary and Joseph with baby Jesus. But wait a minute, while the main characters remain mute and lifeless, baby Jesus appears to be alive and even kicking. The members at Holy Child Jesus (no joke) Church in Queens, New York got the surprise of their lives to discover there was a real-life, new-born baby, so new he was still attached to his umbilical cord, in the scene. He was lying in the manger wrapped in towels. Let's call them 'swaddling clothes' for the sake of authenticity. No one knows how the child came to be part of the Christmas Story, but the vicar and parishioners believe he will be adopted by a loving childless couple making it a great Christmas miracle. Lovely, Jobely!

AND ANOTHER THING...

I believe in God. Where I come from, you had to. And even when I was old enough to make up my own mind I still chose to believe. God has been good to me although there were times I fell out with him. One friend of mine used to say I said that as if I fell out with a neighbour! There were times when it felt like God had dropped my file behind the filing cabinet and forgot where he put it. But in the end he always came through. So it is refreshing to know that after all the forces that tried to persuade and drive home the evolution over creation argument, a recent study by Newham University in Birmingham found that a high percentage of people do not believe in evolution after all. They believe God created man directly as in the story of Adam and Eve. And it's not just religious people who cast doubts over Darwin's theory, but also people who claim to be non-religious.

When catastrophe strikes I never hear anyone say, "May Darwin help us." In fact, during the recent Hurricane Irma which battered the Caribbean, a very pleading headline in a British newspaper said, "May God protect us all", referring to a statement uttered by officials in the affected region. In my experience, faced with situations when my back was against the wall and a rock in front of me, it wasn't man I called out to, but God.

***

A man got caught shoplifting in a grocery store. At court the judge said, 'Sir, I understand you stole a can of peaches. How many peaches were in that can?' 'Five, your honour.' The man replied.

The judge said, 'Alright, I'm going to give you one week in jail for each peach. You get five weeks.' Just then the man's wife stood up. 'Your honour, may I say something.' 'Yes, what is it?' The judge asked. 'He stole a can of peas too!' She offered.

Walk good!

Dedication

This book is also dedicated to all girls who were victims of abuse, yet through an invincible spirit survived and grew into amazing women whose light shines brighter and brighter with each passing day.

Ninety per cent of the profits of the sales of this book will go to charities supporting these victims to victory.

Acknowledgements

I owe special thanks to the brilliant Errol Lloyd, Writer and Artist, whose helping hand, insight and guidance in this project has been invaluable and to Cheryl Lanyon for her par excellent editorial and organisational work. Thanks also to my dear friend Jeannie McPherson for her unwavering support and belief in me and this book; gratitude to my spiritual sister-friend Pauline Phillips who has had cause to stand in the gap on my behalf on far too many occasions. And to my wonderful friends who showed tremendous interest in this project and cheered me along. Thank you.

About the Author

In real life, J.A. Lovelock JP, is a Barrister-at-Law of Middle Temple and an alumna of The Inns of Court School of Law. As an academic lawyer and lecturer, she has spent a career in legal education which included training, examining and consultancy on an international scale. She has Bachelor's degrees in law, in Criminology and in Social Policy. She also earned a Masters degree in Law. She was a candidate for the Professional Doctorate in Criminal Justice at Portsmouth University Institute of Criminal Justice Studies (which she forsook to have more fun!).

At play, she is a television and award-winning radio presenter and producer. Her non-fiction writing has appeared in *The Lawyer, The Gleaner UK* and *The Voice*. She also spent some time producing and publishing her own magazine in London. Her fiction has been shortlisted in national competitions and some are published in *Turf* and anthology for new writers. Apart from writing she loves to sing and has appeared in critically acclaimed productions at Hackney Empire Theatre, the Orange Tree Theatre, Richmond, Surrey and the Tricycle Theatre, Kilburn.

Born in Kingston, Jamaica, she currently resides in the United Kingdom.

Contact J.A. Lovelock at

ja@jalovelock.com

*Available worldwide from Amazon
and all good bookstores*

―――――――

http://mtp.agency

http://facebook.com/mtp.agency

@mtp_agency

www.ingramcontent.com/pod-product-compliance
Lightning Source LLC
LaVergne TN
LVHW012113070526
838202LV00056B/5714